Contents

Acknowledgements

I would like to say thank you to my husband John for his continued support and encouragement; to Gina Ashman for reviewing the book for me; and Nina Stibbe, of David Fulton Publishers, for her enthusiasm for the project from start to finish.

I am also grateful to *Nursery World* for agreeing to publish the Jasmine Maya column in the first place and for supporting its extension within this text.

A huge thank you is especially due to Jasmine's parents for allowing me to continue to follow her development, and for keeping me informed of any new words and achievements as and when they occur.

To my late father, Sidney Powton, who would have been a wonderful grandad and great-grandad.

And to Jasmine, my granddaughter, an absolute joy to have around.

Introduction

This illustrated guide to the development of infants from birth until their second birthday offers a specific focus on a unique stage in the human lifespan. Not only have the developmental changes and stages been noted, but some of the factors that influence development are also examined, enabling the reader to understand more fully some of the causes and effects that life, circumstances and genetics can have.

The extensive use of visual material, which has been set out in such a way as to be informative, interesting and inviting, will form a useful point of reference for both early years students and practitioners, and also for parents of young children.

As with any book discussing development, the stages of normative development set out in this text are purely averages, and it is important that this is kept in mind. Few children develop according to all the 'norms', some leaping ahead and some taking a little longer to reach each milestone. Most children will fall into the category of being a little ahead of the norms in one area of development, but a little behind in another. Again this will vary in individual children as they grow.

Students on a range of early years courses will find this book helpful in extending and consolidating their understanding of how babies and toddlers develop, what can affect their development and also how to care for them. Practical information is given, with diagrams where appropriate.

The unique feature of the book is the inclusion of a 'real' child's development throughout, taking the theory and discussion of a textbook and firmly rooting it in reality. The child discussed here is Jasmine, whom many readers will recognise as the baby featured within a monthly column in *Nursery World* magazine, which followed her development since she was born. Jasmine is a classic example of how a child is advanced in one area of development but takes longer in another. She really adds a personality to the text.

A month in the life of Jasmine Maya

Part five: four months old

During her fourth month Jasmine has developed more strength in her forearms and begun to push herself up when prone. She still shows enjoyment when propped up against cushions and looks around with interest, listening intensely to household noises. If offered a rattle, she will hold it firmly and shake it vigorously. Her movements have limited control as yet and she needs supervision to prevent her hitting herself.

Jasmine is fascinated with mobiles, watching them closely and showing excitement by jerky body movements. She responds to anything that dangles and all tactile experiences, clearly showing pleasure at satin ribbons being stroked across her cheeks, her mouth rooting for them as they pass.

When supine, Jasmine has discovered how to bang her feet up and down, which amuses her greatly. She chuckles and coos, conversationally with familiar adults, smiling at anyone who gives her attention, including the family pets.

As she reached four months she was introduced to solid food. This first consisted purely of baby rice made with expressed breast milk, but was followed in a few days by potato mixed with gluten-free gravy and stewed apple (without sugar). Jasmine seemed to enjoy the sensation of solids and soon managed to co-ordinate her tongue and mouth actions for the spoon. Her mother offered her cooled boiled water in a feeder cup, but she was unsure how to suck from it. She will not accept a bottle at all.

Questions

1. Why are solid foods introduced from around four months of age?
2. Why is it recommended that babies are given gluten-free foods for the first six months?
3. What precautions should be taken regarding pets when there is a baby around?

Answers to part four questions: (16 August)

1. It is standard practice to refer a baby to a GP or a paediatrician if weight continues to cause concern, and they are automatically referred if their weight crosses two centile lines in either direction.
2. Massage is a tactile experience that plays an important part in the bonding process of many parent/child relationships as they are focusing fully on each other and making eye contact.
3. The triple immunisation protects against diphtheria, whooping cough and tetanus. Hib protects against one particular strain of meningitis.

By Sandy Green, an early years lecturer and Jasmine's grandmother

A month in the life of Jasmine Maya

Part nine: eight months old

As Jasmine approached eight months she attended her developmental check with her health visitor. She was declared healthy and developing well, although still small for her age and birth weight, being just above the 2nd centile at 6.69kg (14lb 12 1/2oz).

Jasmine's mobility has increased greatly during this month. She is crawling well in all directions and is able to sit herself up from a crawling position. She is occasionally seen 'bear walking' on her hands and feet too.

Vocally, Jasmine has added the sounds 'bababa' and 'ayoh' to her vocabulary. She is very vocal now, making a huge range of sounds at different pitches, and discovering the pleasure of squealing high and loud, laughing to herself as she listens.

Jasmine currently prefers finger foods to being spoon-fed, and her mother now presents her meals in small, soft pieces, which she can handle well. Having always been breast-fed, Jasmine has refused water in a bottle, and until now has not coped well with a cup, but she has finally mastered the skill of drinking water from her beaker and drinks quite well with her meals.

Jasmine shows great interest in picture books, looking at them repeatedly and patting the pages with pleasure. She favours particular toys now, returning to them again and again, and always smiles at certain objects – her 'teething bunny' and a dog that barks.

Questions

1. At what age would you usually replace a baby's milk feed with water to accompany their meals?
2. As a baby becomes more mobile, what safety issues would you need to consider?
3. Jasmine's mother has prepared her a 'treasure basket'. What is this?

Answers to part eight questions (20/27 Dec)

1. Babies love pictures of other babies. Research has shown that they respond to faces more than any other pattern or shape, an early indication of the need for social interaction.
2. Babies begin to move around from about six months of age, often backwards on their tummies (commando style). Traditional crawling occurs mostly from around eight months.
3. Ideal first finger foods would include slices of banana, fingers of lightly toasted bread, pieces of ripe pear, unsweetened rusks or baby rice cakes.

By Sandy Green, an early years consultant and freelance trainer. She is also Jasmine's grandmother

A month in the life of Jasmine Maya

Part 20: 19 months old

During this month of Jasmine's life, fine weather has let her spend much of her time outdoors, giving her the opportunity to practise her new favourite word – 'flower', which she pronounces 'flaa'. Everywhere Jasmine goes, she notices and points to flowers. She likes to stop and admire each one, repeating 'flaa' over and over. A walk down the garden can take some time!

Jasmine likes to play ball and can kick one, without force, while keeping her balance. She loves to be chased, often initiating this game by running and squealing, looking over her shoulder at her pursuer. She picks daisies and blows on them, and knows that she is not to touch the planted flowers. Jasmine enjoys a special game with Granny, under the flower arch, pointing alternatively at 'Jasmine person and jasmine flower', giggling with pleasure.

Jasmine has a watering can, but waters herself more than the flowers. Given the opportunity, she plays with water with enthusiasm, soaking everything nearby. The dumper truck she enjoyed on the beach last month is now used to collect leaves, daisies and fallen apples from the garden.

Indoors Jasmine enjoys placing all her stacking beakers inside each other and building bricks one on top of the other. Although she can manage three or four quite easily, she currently prefers to take the top one off each time before adding another, never building a tower above two bricks high. She has started to 'stir' a 'cup of coffee' with a plastic key, and enjoys giving her doll a ride on her tricycle.

At the beginning of this month Jasmine was weighed. She is still very petite, weighing 8.6kg (19lb), but is healthy and always full of energy.

Questions

1. In her play Jasmine is beginning to imitate actions she sees. At what age is this most commonly found?
2. What other examples of imitative play would you expect to see Jasmine demonstrate?
3. Jasmine is clearly a lightweight child. What weight would you expect her to be at 18 to 19 months?

Answers to part 19 questions: (21 November)

1. Jasmine eats meals better when listening to tapes or to the radio, because she is concentrating on the music and eating with less focus on the food.
2. Toddlers of this age love to return to the same books over and over. It helps them consolidate their understanding of what they are seeing, while adults reinforce the names of objects for them.
3. Familiar items are an important aspect of all children's lives. It offers them an element of security within their immediate and extended environments.

By Sandy Green, an early years consultant and freelance trainer. She is also Jasmine's grandmother

The full range of Jasmine Maya columns can be accessed at www.sandy-green.com.

Throughout this book there are 'checkpoint' questions which give opportunities for reflection and evaluation of knowledge and understanding. The answers to all the set questions can be found in the Appendix at the back of the book. Aspects of health, safety and developmental psychology have also been included, helping to further raise awareness of the safety needs of this very vulnerable age group, and also to offer some outline ideas regarding what helps children to develop as they do and why.

A glossary of terms has been included, which has allowed the book to provide both a practical and a more academic remit, enabling the use of correct terminology while appealing to a wide audience.

At the back of the book is a 'Reference and further reading' section, giving details of books and articles that have been referred to in the text, and also offering suggestions for further reading on relevant topics.

Note: In an effort to avoid confusion, the pronoun 'he' has been used for infants in general throughout, leaving 'she' for use in references to Jasmine, her mummy, and to mothers in general.

Introduction to Jasmine

Jasmine Maya was born in January 2001. At the time of writing she is a typical two-year-old – cuddly, energetic, full of smiles, and always up to mischief.

Jasmine was a small for dates, full-term infant weighing 2.780 kg (6 lb 2 oz), which placed her just below the ninth centile for weight on her development record. At age two she is still very petite, but with a voice inconsistent with her tiny size!

Jasmine loves climbing and adores animals, particularly cows, ducks and cats. Some of her favourite toys are Megablocks, footballs, shopping bags and books, but she also loves her soft toys. Jasmine, who is rarely still, enjoys running, climbing and dancing. She can be seen bobbing to and fro to any source of music. She is a sociable little girl who clearly enjoys being with people, most of all her parents and her extended family. She is also confident with children and adults at toddler groups and activity centres. At the time of going to press, Jasmine had recently become a big sister. Prior to the birth of her brother, Harry, she practiced hard with her dolly which she calls 'Beebee' (baby).

Jasmine aged 19 months

Observation

Observation of an infant means watching the child carefully in an informed way. As you observe you automatically increase your understanding of developmental patterns and individual personality traits. As a parent, observation is predominantly used for pleasure and for reassurance that a child is happy, healthy and developing well. As an early years student or practitioner there is the additional focus of professional knowledge development, and close observation is used as a means of assessment.

Observation can take many forms. It can be either specific (focusing on one aspect of development in particular, for example language), or it can be generalised (simply noting all aspects of a child's development at a given time). It can also be planned or spontaneous.

Observation is an important and mandatory part of any course of study in early years.

Observing Jasmine

As Jasmine's grandmother I have been privileged to share regularly in her life, living in the same house with her during her first few months and seeing her at least twice each week since then. Jasmine's parents have generously given me permission to record and photograph Jasmine whenever I wish, and this has enabled me to draw up an extensive record of each aspect of her development. This has been a wonderful experience both personally and professionally, and I am extremely grateful to have had such an opportunity.

Pregnancy, birth and the neonate

Pregnancy and foetal development

Beginnings

The zygote

Once conception has taken place and the fertilised ovum has implanted itself in the wall of the uterus, the outer layers of this cluster of cells begin to form the placenta, while the inner cells will develop into the baby. From conception to implantation this developing 'being' is referred to as a 'zygote'.

Following implantation the term used changes to 'embryo'. The embryo develops within an amniotic sac (see Figure 1.1).

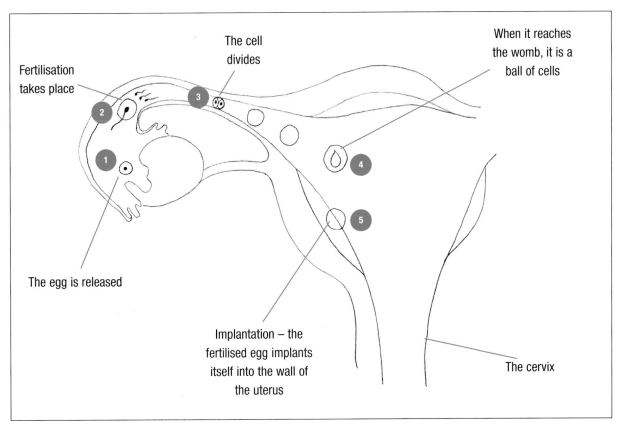

Figure 1.1   From conception to implantation

The amniotic sac

The amniotic sac is made up of two thin layers of tissue. The outer layer (the chorion) and the inner layer (the amnion). It is the muscular bag of fluid in which the embryo develops. Its four main functions are to:

● maintain a constant temperature
● protect the embryo from shock and knocks
● help to prevent infection
● give the embryo freedom of movement.

The amniotic fluid

Amniotic fluid is made up of water, salts, fats, and later on foetal urine too. At 16 weeks there is approximately 250 ml (9 fl oz) of fluid, and by 22 weeks there is approximately 800 ml (29 fl oz) of fluid, which remains stable until around 39 weeks when it begins to reduce. By delivery, fluid levels have usually dropped to at least 500 ml (18 fl oz), but are lower if the delivery is delayed. Amniotic fluid absorbs foetal waste throughout the pregnancy. It is swallowed and passed by the foetus (the term used from eight weeks onwards). Fluid levels are monitored during both routine and specific ultrasound scans, as lack of sufficient fluid can indicate a potential problem in some pregnancies. Information on ultrasound scans can be found on page 10.

The neural tube

The neural tube begins to form from the end of the third week, as the central nervous system of the embryo starts to develop. Its outer layer is called the ectoderm (forming skin, brain and nerves).

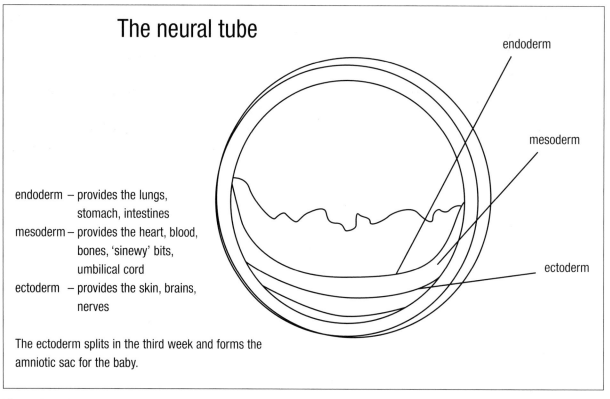

Figure 1.2   A cross-section of the neural tube roll

As Figure 1.2 shows, if viewed as a cross-section the next (inner) layer is the 'mesoderm' (forming heart, blood, bones, 'sinewy' bits and umbilical cord), and the most central layer is the 'endoderm' (forming the lungs, stomach and intestines).

The embryo

By week four, arm and leg buds are visible and the heart begins to beat. By six weeks, finger buds are beginning to develop (see Figure 1.3), although the arms are still very short. Both the heart and liver can now be identified with specialist equipment. Between six and eight weeks the vertebrae, which will protect the already developing spinal cord, are forming, and at eight weeks the term used changes from 'embryo' to 'foetus'.

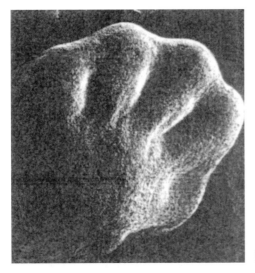

Figure 1.3 Finger buds

The foetus

Everything that the infant is going to have at birth has now been established. Foetal development is a stage of growth in which detail is completed, building on the earlier (embryo) stage of formation. The muscles have started to work already and by 12 weeks the limbs are constantly moving. The sex organs are well developed and soft nails and teeth are now forming.

By 20 weeks the foetus can suck and grip. He has been able to hear for some time now and will be making strong movements that can usually be felt by the mother. By 22 weeks the foetus is covered with a soft downy hair called 'lanugo', and by 24 weeks a protective substance secreted by the sebaceous glands ('vernix caseosa') coats the skin. The mother may be able to identify sleep patterns now in her unborn infant (Figure 1.4).

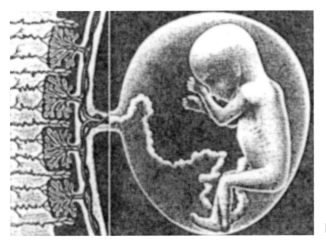

Figure 1.4 An infant in the womb

At 28 weeks the foetus is usually considered to be medically 'viable'. This means that the main physiological systems (for breathing, the nervous system and circulation) are usually well enough developed for a reasonable chance of survival if the baby is delivered early for any reason. The foetus would now be around 23 cm (9 inches) in length and weighing around 1.220 kg (2 lb 10 oz).

By 36 weeks, most infants are positioned for birth with the head well down. Delivery of a full-term infant usually takes place at around 40 weeks.

Jasmine's development in the womb

Jasmine's development in the womb was confirmed early in her mother's pregnancy, enabling her to start taking folic acid immediately (see page 9 for information on the benefits of folic acid). The pregnancy was described as 'unremarkable', since there were no causes for concern and no relevant family or medical history to take into account.

It was a first pregnancy for Jasmine's mother, who is of a slight build. Although she initially lost weight rather than gaining it, due to pregnancy sickness, she eventually gained weight healthily. Her sickness lasted until around 20 weeks and she was given an iron supplement to improve her lowered haemoglobin levels. Routine blood and urine tests were carried out without any unusual outcomes and ultrasound scans were taken at 20 weeks (Figure 1.5) and then again at 37 weeks.

At 20 weeks the routine ultrasound scan showed that Jasmine's bone development and head circumference gave a reading of 19 + 5 weeks' gestation. The amniotic fluid levels indicated 19 + 1 weeks. According to her own dates, Jasmine's mother was 19 + 3 weeks pregnant, therefore the scan indicated that the foetus (Jasmine) was developing well within normal parameters.

Towards the end of her pregnancy Jasmine's mother's weight gain ceased and a scan at 37 weeks was used to check that all was well, which it was.

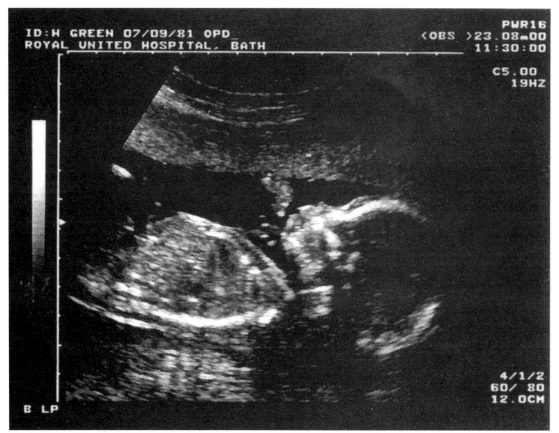

Figure 1.5   An ultrasound scan of Jasmine at 20 weeks

Factors that can influence development before birth

There are many factors which can affect an infant before birth, and even prior to conception. If a pregnancy is planned the woman can help prepare her body so that the optimum environment for a pregnancy is created, for example by giving up smoking, avoiding alcohol altogether (or at the very least reducing it to a minimum), avoiding the use of drugs – prescribed, over-the-counter, or recreational – and eating healthily. Getting sufficient fresh air and rest is also beneficial.

Taking a folic acid supplement helps provide for optimum central nervous system development and is recommended from before conception (or as soon as pregnancy is suspected) up to three months into the pregnancy.

Table 1.1   Effects of smoking, alcohol and drugs on foetal development

Substance	Potential effects on developing foetus
Smoking (tobacco and other substances)	Low birth-weight is common due to nicotine being released into the body Can also lead to learning difficulties Thought to be a possible link to sudden infant death syndrome (also known as SIDs or cot death)
Alcohol	Foetal alcohol syndrome (FAS) is caused by women consuming large quantities of alcohol during pregnancy. FAS causes developmental delay, learning difficulties and deformities Alcohol can impair judgement and increase the risk of accidents
Drugs	Drugs such as cocaine cause low birth-weight and developmental delay Infants can be born addicted and suffer terrible withdrawal symptoms All round development problems are common, together with epilepsy Drugs are always prescribed with care to pregnant women to avoid complications It should be remembered that cough and cold remedies are also drugs and their suitability should be checked with a GP or pharmacist All non-essential drugs should be avoided during pregnancy

Eating well during pregnancy helps ensure that both mother and child have sufficient nutrients. It is also wise for pregnant women to avoid foods such as soft cheeses and pâtés which occasionally contain listeria, a bacterium that can cause miscarriage, and also foods made with raw eggs, such as home-made mayonnaise and chocolate mousse, which can potentially cause salmonella food poisoning.

Care should be taken if handling raw meat, as toxoplasmosis can cause serious harm to the developing foetus, causing hydrocephalus (inflammation of the brain), blindness, enlargement of the liver and spleen, and severe learning difficulties. Furthermore, it can cause miscarriage or stillbirth. It is also sensible for women in the early months of pregnancy to avoid visits to farms or animal centres during the lambing season, again to reduce the risk of infection and possible miscarriage.

Screening in pregnancy

Tests carried out during a woman's pregnancy are part of the general health screening programme offered to people in most countries across Western society. Some tests are considered to be routine and are offered to all women. Others are used where a pregnant woman is considered to be in a high-risk category, or where a concern or potential problem has already been identified.

This may include women whose family or partner's family have a history of genetically inherited disorders, or be when a woman is considered (medically) to be an older mother. The tests included in screening are listed below.

Blood tests

Routine blood tests screen for low iron levels, sexually transmitted disease and rubella (German measles). Iron supplements are recommended if haemoglobin (iron) levels are low, and sexually transmitted diseases will be treated in the relevant way. A pregnant woman who is not immune to rubella is always advised to avoid contact with anyone who has the infection during the early months of her pregnancy as it can cause serious hearing and vision defects in the unborn infant.

Ultrasound scan

An ultrasound scan is a routine procedure at around 20 weeks into the pregnancy (at 20 weeks' gestation) noting the development levels and measurements of the foetus. Measurements are taken of main bones such as the femur (thigh bone), and the head circumference. The heart chambers are also carefully examined. If any potential problems are identified, further scans are carried out as is considered necessary by the midwife or obstetrician.

The foetus featured in Figures 1.5 and 1.6 (this was Jasmine) is developing within the normal range. Measurements and examinations were made of the:

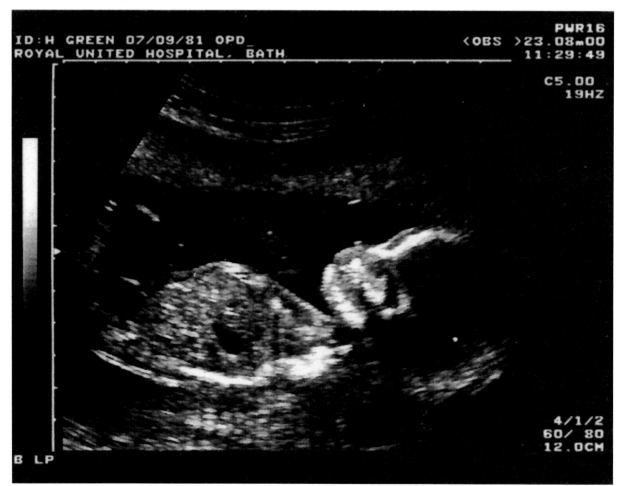

Figure 1.6 A scan of Jasmine as a 20-week foetus

- thigh bone
- head circumference
- spine
- heart chambers
- brain
- amniotic fluid.

The outcome showed that the foetus (Jasmine) had bone development and a head circumference that indicated 19 + 5 weeks of gestation, and amniotic fluid associated with 19 + 1 weeks' gestation. These results showed that the foetus was developing well within normal limits, as Jasmine's mother's pregnancy was at 19 + 3 weeks, according to her own dates.

Serum alpha-fetoprotein (SAFP)

This test is usually carried out at 16 weeks' gestation and is offered to women who are considered to be at risk of having a child with spina bifida.

The triple blood test

This triple blood test is offered to women in the high-risk group, usually mothers over 35 years. It takes into consideration the mother's age, together with measurements of human chorionic gonadotrophin (HCG) levels, Serum alpha-fetoprotein (SAFP) and the placental hormones (oestriols). The outcome of combining these pieces of information gives an assessment of any risk that the foetus may have Down's syndrome.

Amniocentesis

An amniocentesis test checks for chromosome disorders, such as Down's syndrome. It is usually carried out between 16 and 18 weeks of pregnancy and involves taking a sample of the amniotic fluid from the amniotic sac while the mother is linked up to an ultrasound machine. The link enables the procedure to be carried out with as much visibility as possible. There is a slight risk of miscarriage occurring with this procedure.

Chorionic villi sampling (CVS)

Chorionic villi sampling involves the direct removal of a tiny amount of tissue from the placenta. It is a procedure usually carried out between 8 and 11 weeks' gestation when a mother is considered to be at risk. It can help identify a range of inherited disorders, but, as with the amniocentesis procedure, it also carries a risk of miscarriage.

Genetics

Genetic inheritance is a major influence on development, and for most newborn infants it is simply the inheritance of characteristics of their parents that are noticeably passed down. These observable characteristics are known by the term 'phenotype'.

Another genetic term is 'genotype', which is used to describe the full genetic inheritance of the infant. This includes any genetically inherited disorders.

Genetically inherited disorders

There are three categories of genetically inherited disorders. They are known as:

- autosomal dominant transference
- autosomal recessive transference
- X-linked transference.

Table 1.2 The three types of transference

Type of transference	Chance of condition being passed on to the child	Typical family tree of condition
Autosomal dominant	1 in 2 chance	
Autosomal recessive	1 in 4 chance	
X-linked	Condition is passed by the X chromosome, so boys are affected and girls are carriers of the condition	

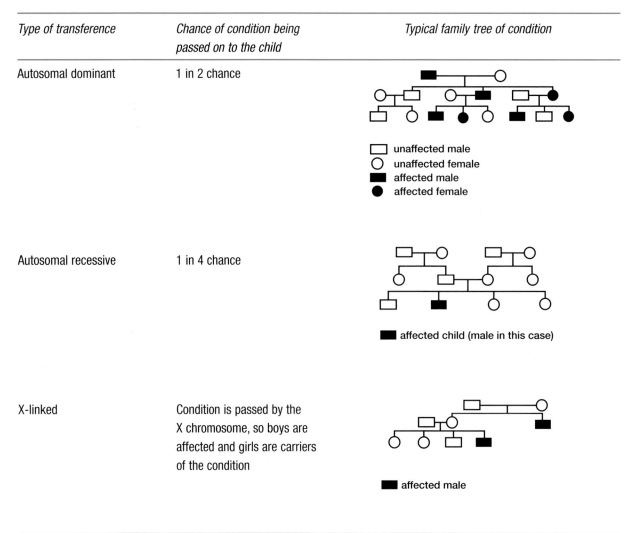

unaffected male
unaffected female
affected male
affected female

affected child (male in this case)

affected male

JASMINE

Jasmine: a summary of relevant pre-birth factors

Jasmine's mother did not smoke and rarely drank alcohol. She took only the occasional paracetamol for a headache and started taking folic acid as soon as she suspected she was pregnant.

Having registered her pregnancy with her GP she kept her appointments with primary care staff (GP, midwife and health visitor) as appropriate. As she was both young and healthy and there was no family or medical history of any concern, no tests other than routine ones were made.

To avoid any possibility of complication from toxocariasis Jasmine's mother was particularly careful to wash her hands after handling the family pets, and was not involved in clearing away dog faeces from the garden or during walks throughout her pregnancy.

Jasmine's mother opted for a midwife delivery within the maternity suite of a large hospital, followed by a couple of days rest at a small 'local' maternity unit. This gave her access to the full range of medical interventions in the event of any complications during delivery, with the calm, supportive atmosphere of a more homely environment afterwards.

Birth

Trimesters

A woman's pregnancy is made up of three trimesters, dividing it into three periods of three months. During the first trimester (up to around 14 weeks) the foetus forms all the aspects of its body that it will have at birth, and during this period the woman often experiences a range of symptoms such as nausea and vomiting, frequency of urination and fatigue.

During the second trimester (up to around 28 weeks) the foetus continues to grow and develop and the mother is often found to be enjoying her pregnancy. Having gone past much of the early discomfort, she now mostly feels quite well.

By the third trimester (up to full term, i.e. 40 weeks) the foetus is termed 'viable' and is quite well formed, standing a chance of survival outside the womb if born early.

Labour

The onset of labour is sometimes preceded by the sudden release of the plug of mucus at the neck of the womb. Some women experience their waters breaking as a constant trickle, but occasionally it happens with a whoosh! For most women, labour starts with a dull backache, caused by the uterus beginning to contract. As labour intensifies, contractions become stronger and more frequent until eventually the infant is ready to be born.

Labour is generally divided into three stages:

- The first stage is measured from the onset of contractions until the cervix is fully dilated and ready to deliver the infant.
- The second stage involves the actual delivery of the infant.
- The third stage sees the delivery of the placenta, which is checked to ensure that it is intact and no part of it has remained inside the mother, risking the onset of infection.

Birth is exciting, painful and often exhausting for the mother. It is probably an infant's most dangerous journey too. Contrasting birth options include a hospital delivery, a midwife delivery within the maternity suite, or a home birth. Unless there are medical reasons to indicate otherwise, it is the mother's choice that will be upheld as far as is practicable.

Birth can vary from being completely natural, with the mother finding her own position and managing without pain relief or gas and air, through to the medical intervention of an epidural, forceps, ventouse suction or caesarian delivery, as shown in Table 1.3.

Table 1.3 Medical interventions during birth

Type of intervention	What it involves	Reasons for it
Epidural	Anaesthesia via injection or through continuous administration by catheter, usually placed in the lumbar region of the mother's spine.	Pain relief and non-emergency caesarian
Forceps	The easing out of the infant with forceps (flat tong-shaped 'tool')	Foetal distress requiring a prompt delivery; a 'stuck' infant; infant in an abnormal position
Ventouse suction	A disc-shaped cup is attached to the infant's skull and a vacuum is created by a pump, which draws out the air, enabling extraction in time with the mother's contraction	To ease delivery
Caesarian	Delivery through an incision made in the abdominal wall	Foetal distress; infant in difficult presentation; too large an infant for vaginal delivery; medical emergency

Women are encouraged to write a birth plan, indicating what their preferences are regarding pain relief and delivery. Some women are able to keep to their birth plan, but many abandon the idea of a 'natural' birth, entirely free from pain relief, once the contractions really get going!

Immediately after the birth, the infant is assessed using the Apgar score chart (a series of assessments devised by Dr Virginia Apgar), as shown in Table 1.4.

Table 1.4 The Apgar score chart

Sign	0	1	2
Heart rate	Absent	<100 beats per minute	>100 beats per minute
Respiration	Absent	Slow, irregular	Good, regular
Muscle tone	Limp	Some flexion of extremities	Active
Response to stimulus (stimulation of foot or nose)	No response	Grimace	Cry, cough
Colour	Blue, pale	Body oxygenated, bluish extremities	Well-oxygenated, completely pink

This chart enables a quick assessment of a newborn's well-being, giving the infant a score out of ten.

Vitamin K

With parental consent all newborn infants are given Vitamin K at birth to prevent the rare but very dangerous condition called 'neonatal haemorrhage'. It can be given either via an injection, or orally.

Birth-weight

The average weight at birth is 3.175 kg (7 lb) for a girl and 3.4 kg (7½ lb) for a boy. Weight, length and head circumference are plotted on centile (or percentile) charts (see Figure 1.7). They give an average, and an average range, within which 80 per cent of infants will be placed.

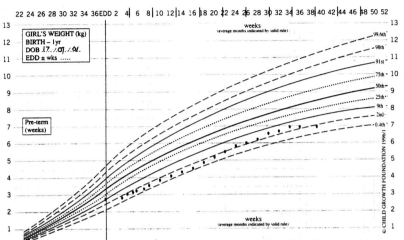

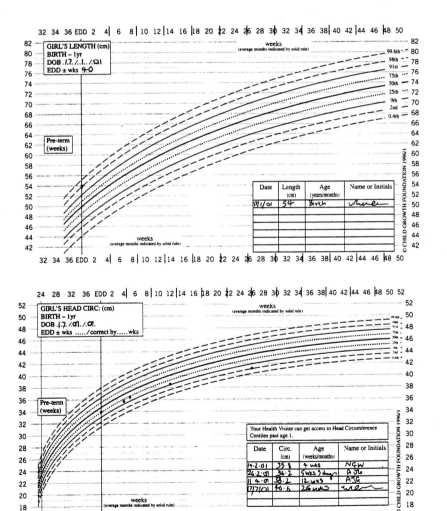

Figure 1.7 Examples of centile charts for weight, length and head circumference

Jasmine's birth and her mother's labour

Jasmine was born after a 14-hour labour. Her mother's waters broke in the early hours of the morning and contractions started immediately. Having controlled the pain with her breathing and with gas and air for a few hours, her mother then had a pethadine injection to help with pain relief. The baby, however, was taking her time and eventually an epidural was also administered and Jasmine was delivered by ventouse suction. Her head had been tilted forward, making delivery difficult, but one quick suction enabled her to arrive safely and be placed onto her mother.

Once her head had been delivered and while waiting for the next contraction to deliver the rest of her body, Jasmine had her eyes wide open and was looking around, much to the amusement of all those present. As Jasmine's grandmother (also present at her birth) I was given the honour of cutting the umbilical cord and welcoming her into the world. Jasmine was then put to her mother's breast.

Although wide awake and having given a lusty cry, Jasmine was not immediately interested in sucking and did not root for the breast.

She weighed 2.780 kg (6 lb 2 oz), which was considered to be 'light for dates' (she was placed just below the ninth centile). Her length was 54 cm (98th centile), and her head circumference was 34 cm (just above the 25th centile).

Jasmine scored 9 out of 10 on the Apgar score chart at both one minute and five minutes old. Her extremities remained slightly bluish in colour. She was quite a 'mucky' baby, coated with mucus and vernix caseosa, and her mother agreed to the midwife giving her a quick bath when she was just one hour old. Jasmine appeared calm and content throughout her bath.

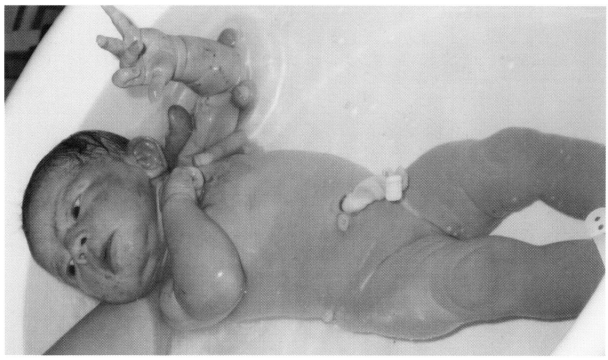

Jasmine having her first bath

Jasmine was given a Vitamin K injection when she was one and a half hours old with her parents' consent.

As Jasmine was considered to be small for dates her blood sugar levels were automatically checked every three hours. They were slightly low and she was also quite 'jittery'. At approximately seven hours old she was briefly taken down to the SCBU (special care baby unit) to be assessed by a paediatrician, but was soon allowed back to the maternity ward.

Infant deaths

Sadly, despite the high standards of care and medical intervention available today, a small number of infants still die. They are categorised officially and medically according to the time at which death takes place. The categories are:

- *Stillbirth*: any infant who dies before birth and after the 24th week of pregnancy is officially termed as being a stillborn infant.
- *Perinatal death*: a term used to describe an infant whose death occurs within one week of birth. Within official figures, the perinatal mortality rate also includes the numbers of babies who have been stillborn.
- *Neonatal death*: a term used to describe infants who die within the first 28 days after birth.
- *Post-neonatal death*: children who die following the 28th day of their life, but before they reach their first birthday, are placed in the category of post-neonatal deaths.

Physical appearance of an infant at birth

For the first month of life an infant is referred to as a 'neonate'. The physical appearance of each individual neonate will be determined by his genes, but there are certain features that are common to all neonates, including those listed below:

A lack of head control

A lack of head control is often referred to as 'head lag'. It is due to the neck muscles being immature and therefore the infant's head and neck need to be well supported whenever he is being handled (see Figure 1.8).

Figure 1.8 A baby with head lag and a well-supported infant

Vernix caseosa

This is a creamy white substance that covers the unborn infant in the womb. It protects and lubricates the skin and is usually still seen on pre-term babies, and often on full-term infants too. An example of vernix caseosa can be seen in the photograph of Jasmine having her first bath aged just one hour, on page 16.

Lanugo

Lanugo is a very soft downy hair that is formed in the womb. It covers the whole of the unborn infant's body following the whorls of the baby's skin surface (see Figure 1.9). Traces are often found on the shoulders, back and ears, particularly if an infant is born before his due date.

Figure 1.9 Lanugo following the whorled pattern

Spots and rashes

Skin irritations such as spots and rashes are common in newborn infants. Small white spots known as 'milia' (or 'milk spots') are the most frequently found. They last just a short time and usually clear up on their own.

Head shape

An infant's head can be slightly flattened or otherwise misshapen following delivery. It can be due simply to pressure generated as the infant passes through the birth canal, or through the use of forceps or the ventouse suction cap in an assisted delivery. In a multiple birth, lack of space can sometimes leave an infant slightly squashed. An infant's head shape will return to 'normal' within a few weeks and is not usually a cause for concern.

Fontanelles

Newborn infants have two fontanelles (see Figure 1.10). These are areas of the skull where the bony plates have not yet fused together. This allows for a little movement during the birth. The 'anterior fontanelle' is diamond-shaped and is positioned near to the front of the skull. It closes over by around 18 months. The 'posterior fontanelle' is a small triangular area found near to the crown and this closes over within a few weeks of birth. The fontanelles pulsate with the infant's heartbeat and this can sometimes be clearly seen. If the fontanelles appear to be sunken it may indicate that the infant is in need of a greater level of fluids. If they appear to be bulging it can indicate increased pressure around the brain, or an infection, in which case an urgent medical assessment will be needed.

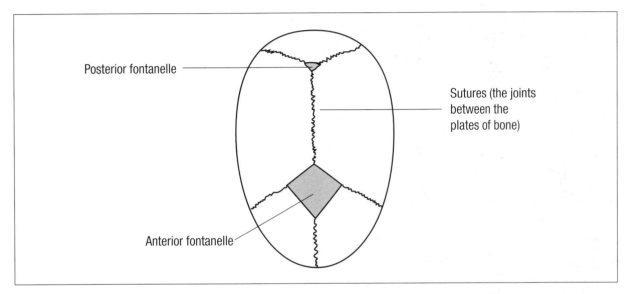

Posterior fontanelle

Sutures (the joints between the plates of bone)

Anterior fontanelle

Figure 1.10   The fontanelles on a baby's skull

Posture

Neonates are usually flexed (curled up) and their movements appear jerky and uncoordinated.

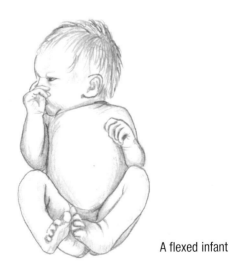

A flexed infant

Poor circulation

A newborn infant's hands and feet are often cool and bluish in colour. This is due to poor circulation in the earliest days and soon improves.

Bruising

Newborn infants sometimes appear bruised. As with misshapen heads, this is due to the birth process and soon disappears.

Eyes

The eyes of neonates are usually uncoordinated and sometimes 'wander' or 'cross' as they try to focus. Some infants have 'sticky' eyes which need careful bathing. Again, this soon clears up. Permanent eye colour is not established for several months.

The umbilical stump

The umbilical cord is clamped immediately after birth and a stump remains where the clamp was attached. This needs to be kept clean and dry, but only actually requires cleaning if and when it becomes mucky. It usually dries out and drops off within a few days.

Effects of the mother's hormones

Sometimes, the mother's hormones can cross the placenta and the effects of them are seen in newborn infants. Indications of this are swollen breasts in both boys and girls, sometimes leaking a little milk; swollen genitals, again in both boys and girls; and a slight vaginal blood loss in girls.

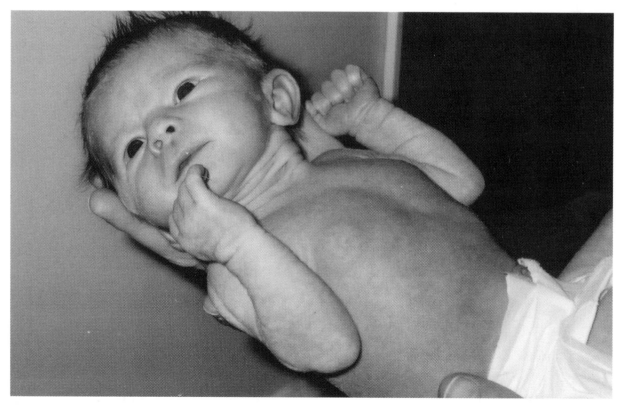

Jasmine with swollen breasts

Dark faeces – meconium

The first faeces (or stools) passed by the neonate are very sticky, like tar. They are dark greenish black in colour and are called 'meconium'. As milk feeding becomes established this changes the colour and consistency of the faeces. The stools of breast-fed babies tend to have a less powerful odour than those of infants receiving formula feeds.

Neonatal jaundice

The immature liver of some infants is unable to cope with its workload and levels of bilirubin are formed. This causes a yellowing of the skin and eyes. It usually occurs around day three after birth, and the infant is sometimes given phototherapy under an ultraviolet light to remedy the problem.

Birthmarks

Birthmarks may be present at the time of birth, or develop shortly after it. Table 1.5 sets out a range of them.

Table 1.5 Different types of birthmarks

Birthmark	Type of mark	Temporary/permanent
Port wine mark	A dark red mark, often on the face or neck	Used to be permanent, but can often be removed or reduced with laser treatment
Strawberry naevus (haemangioma)	A raised mark that appears within a few days of birth, filled with blood vessels	These marks tend to disappear by the age of eight years
'Stork bite' marks	Tiny red marks found on the eyelids, top of the nose and the back of the neck	They gradually disappear
Mongolian blue spot	Dark marks found mostly at the base of the spinal area on dark-skinned infants	Permanent marks that need to be mapped by health professionals to ensure that they are not mistaken for bruising
Congenital melanocytic naevi (CMNs)	Large unsightly moles	These moles get darker as they grow. They can often be removed or reduced with laser treatment

Reflexes

Reflexes are automatic body reactions to certain stimuli. The reflexes seen in the neonate are what are known as 'primary reflexes'. Some of these stay with us for life, while others gradually disappear as more intended reactions are developed. The presence or loss of reflexes indicates the neurological status (and therefore the well-being) of an infant. Primary reflexes include:

- *Blinking*: the infant reacts to sudden noises or light, and to movement in front of his eyes.
- *Sucking*: anything placed in the infant's mouth (for example, a clean finger) will usually be sucked.
- *Rooting*: the infant instinctively turns towards his mother's breast to locate the nipple (he 'roots' for the breast).
- *Palmar grasp*: the infant firmly grasps anything that touches the palm of his hand. The grasp will usually be released if the back of the hand is stroked gently.

Sucking

The palmar grasp

- *Plantar reflex*: an infant will flex his toes towards a finger that touches the sole of his foot.
- *Stepping reflex*: if the infant is held and his foot in allowed to make contact with a firm surface, he will instinctively take a small step.

The stepping reflex

The moro reflex

- *Moro reflex*: any sudden movement of an infant's neck is interpreted by the baby as a falling sensation. This causes the infant to throw his arms outwards with his hands open. He then reclasps his hands over his chest.
- *Startle reflex*: if startled by a sudden noise or movement, the infant again throws his arms outwards, but the hands remain tightly clenched.
- *Asymmetric tonic neck reflex*: if an infant's head is turned to one side, he will automatically respond to this by straightening the arm and leg on the same side, but flexing the limbs of the opposite side.

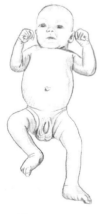

The startle reflex

The asymmetric tonic neck reflex

Importance of monitoring reflexes

An infant's reflexes are a good indicator of neurological well-being. As the brain develops and begins to make more intended decisions, the primitive reflexes begin to disappear. Concerns may be raised if the early reflexes remain longer than the 'norm', possibly indicating that the infant has a neurological problem which will need monitoring.

The senses

Infants learn through the use and stimulation of all of their senses, as illustrated in Figure 1.11. This means they learn through:

- visual experiences (sight)
- auditory experiences (hearing)
- tactile experiences (touch)
- olfactory experiences (smell)
- oral experiences (taste and touch).

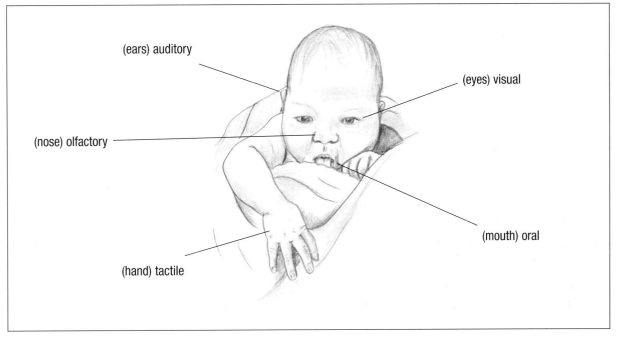

Figure 1.11 Infants learn through their senses

Paediatric checks: following birth

Following birth, an infant is assessed daily by a midwife to ensure that he is well, that feeding becomes established, and that no problems occur. A paediatrician makes a specific assessment of the infant before discharging the baby from hospital (see Figure 1.12). She checks:

- the infant's reflexes, a good indicator of neurological well-being;
- the infant's mouth to ensure that the palate is intact and there are no signs of harelip or tongue tie (a restriction on the movement of the tongue);

- the spine, to ensure it is healthy and straight;
- the hip joints, ensuring that they rotate well and that no signs of clicking hips are present;
- the skull, to ensure it is well formed;
- the heartbeat, to check for any murmurs or other abnormalities;
- the internal organs, to ascertain that they are correctly sized and positioned;
- the testicles of baby boys, feeling for them within the scrotum. If they cannot be found they will be carefully checked again at six weeks.

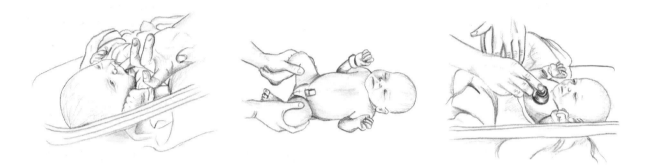

Figure 1.12 Examples of paediatric checks at birth

In some hospitals a neonatal hearing test is now carried out routinely. This can identify hearing problems immediately, enabling support for the infant's auditory system at the earliest opportunity.

The midwife's role

The daily checks by the hospital midwife and the community midwife after discharge from hospital includes the monitoring of the following areas:

- the infant's urine output
- consistency, colour and frequency of stools
- skin blemishes, birthmarks and general skin colour
- feeding positions and the infant's ability to suck
- weight loss (usual in the first few days) and the subsequent weight gain
- the health, and the eventual dropping off, of the umbilical stump.

The midwife also checks the mother's well-being, ensuring that she is recovering both physically and emotionally from the birth of her baby. The midwife usually visits each day until the infant is ten days old, when, providing the cord stump is off, baby is feeding well and putting on weight, and mother and baby are considered to be well, their care is handed over to a health visitor.

The health visitor's role

Between days 11 and 14 the health visitor first visits mother and baby. His or her role is to monitor the infant's general progress, which at this stage is predominantly linked to feeding, sleeping and weight. Topics such as safety, immunisation and cot death are discussed, and advice and help are given regarding feeding positions, settling baby down and coping with older siblings' reactions to the new arrival.

At around day seven or eight, the heel prick test (Guthrie test) is carried out. This tests for two rare conditions: (1) phenylketonuria (PKU), an inherited blood disorder seen in approximately 1 in 10,000 births, which causes learning difficulties and skin problems if left untreated, but can be managed through introducing a strict diet; and (2) hypothyroidism, another serious condition, which is checked through the thyroid stimulating hormone (TSH) test. Any affected infant needs to take a hormone supplement throughout life to alleviate symptoms.

The health visitor will usually visit weekly at first and then extends an open invitation to the family to attend regular clinics where advice can be sought and baby can be weighed. Immunisation programmes (see page 138) are often carried out alongside infant health clinics.

Health visitors can build up quite a close relationship with mothers of young babies. They are one of the best people to identify whether or not the mother is showing any signs of post-natal depression, and are able to offer a listening ear, advice and/or help, and, in the rarest cases, referral as required.

Paediatric checks – at six weeks

An assessment of the infant is made again at around six weeks old. This is often carried out by a paediatrician specialist, but may alternatively be carried out by the family GP. This assessment (see Figure 1.13) checks:

- the size and shape of the baby's skull, always measured with a special non-stretching tape measure;
- the skin, looking for any blemishes, irritations or birthmarks;
- the spine, again checking that it is straight and healthy;
- the infant's muscle tone, checking that movement is symmetrical, and that the head is in line with the body when held forward (in ventral suspension);
- the baby's heartbeat and breathing;
- internal organs, which will again be palpitated in order to ensure the correct positioning of liver, spleen, kidneys and bladder;
- the umbilicus, ensuring that the area where the cord stump had been has dried up well;
- the infant's eyes for signs of cataracts, glaucoma and high blood pressure;
- the infant's sucking reflex, assessed by placing a clean finger in the mouth;
- the palate, again to ensure it is complete;
- the mouth, examining for signs of tongue tie;
- pulses in the main arteries, to ensure that a strong blood supply is circulating the body;
- feet and legs, looking for 'inward turns' or club foot;
- the penis of boys, to ensure that the hole at its tip is correctly positioned;
- the testicles, carefully feeling for them within the scrotum. Occasionally the testes have not descended, and this will be monitored further. They usually descend before the age of three months;
- the vulva in baby girls, a careful examination to check that all parts are correctly sized;
- the hips again, by rotating and pressing them outwards to ensure that 'clicking hips' (a dislocation) is not a problem;
- the reflexes, as the infant's neurological well-being can be assessed by the gradual replacement of reflex actions by specific brain functions, together with the presence of the first social smiles.

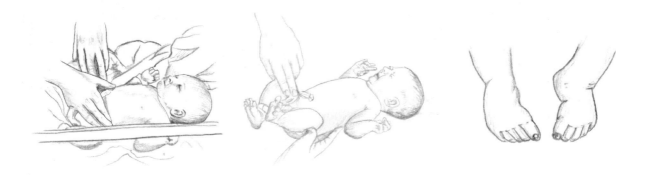

Figure 1.13 Examples of paediatric checks at six weeks

Jasmine's appearance at birth

Jasmine's hair was very dark at birth, with tight curls flat against her skull. Her fingers were noticeably long and her general length was above average. With her weight being below average at 2.780 kg (6 lb 2 oz) she did not have the plumpness often seen in the newborn. She needed to have her name bracelets replaced twice while in hospital, as they slipped over her slim little feet. Jasmine's eyes were dark and she appeared to concentrate hard on whoever she was looking at. At times, her eyes wandered as they lost coordination.

During her first day Jasmine did not feed well at the breast and retched a great deal, bringing up a considerable amount of mucus. Her mother was encouraged to give her a few millilitres of ready-made formula milk via a sterile cup. This also was not very successful. After 24 hours, Jasmine and her mother were able to transfer to a small local maternity unit, and in this peaceful and stress-free environment Jasmine settled, discovered how to suck properly, and breast-feeding was established.

Jasmine had plenty of vernix caseosa on her body at birth (hence the early bath). She had no obvious lanugo present and no sign of spots, blemishes or birthmarks. There was no 'moulding' of her head, and no physical evidence of the ventouse suction cap that helped her delivery. The photograph below shows she liked to lie curled in the flexed foetal position.

Jasmine startled at sudden noises or movements. Her feet and hands remained bluish temporarily while her circulation sorted itself out. Her genitals were typically swollen, as were her breasts, a clear indication that her mother's hormones had crossed the placenta. At four to five days old Jasmine had a slight blood stain in her nappy, again due to the hormone transference from her mother.

By the time Jasmine was taken home by her family on the fourth day her weight had dropped to 2.475 kg (5 lb 8 oz). This was 12 g lower than the 10 per cent loss that is considered to be the healthy 'norm' after birth. This information was passed on to her home-visiting midwife for monitoring.

When Jasmine was lifted across to her first bath by the midwife at one hour old she showed a clear example of the instinctive palmar grasp when she continued to hold onto a small cellular blanket, taking it with her.

The neonatal stage (birth to one month)

During the first month of life (the neonatal stage) infants sleep a great deal, mostly waking for a feed and nappy change. Time spent awake increases gradually week by week and babies become more and more stimulated by the world into which they have been born.

Senses

Sense of vision

Initially infants' vision is diffuse and their range of focus is limited to around 30 cm (12 inches). They blink rapidly in response to both light and sound, and will turn towards a bright light. Research has shown that infants prefer to look at a human face more than any other visual object. Fantz (1961) concluded that this preference for looking at a human face is innate. He found that babies as young as four days old preferred to look at the picture of a normal face (Figure 1.14). The establishment of infant/mother bonding is helped through early eye-to-eye contact between the two.

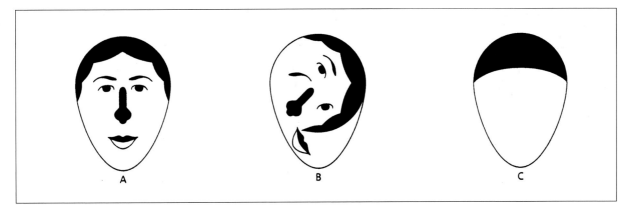

Figure 1.14 Fantz's faces (Reproduced with permission of Nelson Thornes Ltd from *Psychology for You* – Cullis, Dolan and Groves – ISBN 07487 36271 first published 1999)

Sense of hearing

Newborn infants have very acute hearing. They respond well to soothing sounds, particularly sounds with a rhythm, but they become distressed by loud or sudden noises. Almost from birth infants are able to identify and locate the voice of their mother (or main carer).

Sense of touch

The initial skin-to-skin contact made at birth when an infant is delivered onto the mother's abdomen is an important aspect of bonding. For most infants, being handled by their carers is a soothing experience.

an infant being soothed by handling

Sense of smell

The individual body smell of the mother is easily identified by an infant. Infants would also appear to be able to distinguish between their mother's milk and other breast milk when presented with a range of breast pads.

The oral sense

Oral sense covers both taste and touch, with the infant taking in information regarding shape, texture, density and taste by mouthing and sucking objects.

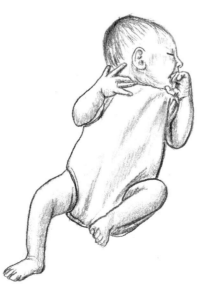

Posture

During the first month infants remain in a naturally flexed posture with hands strongly fisted. They need to be well supported whenever they are being handled.

Hands remain strongly fisted

When supine (laid on their back) there is a tendency for their feet and legs to be raised up, whereas when prone (laid on their tummy) the knees tend to be tucked under and the head turns to one side.

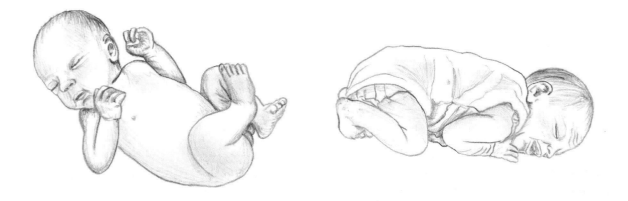

Some newborn infants can be remarkably active, stretching their limbs and turning from side to side, whereas others remain quite still. These early movements start to exercise muscles in the baby's body.

Feeding

Whether being fed by breast or formula, feeding is usually well established within a few days. Breast-feeding is the best option for the infant, as the milk is naturally 'sterile', has the correct nutritional makeup for the infant (often referred to as nature's 'designer' food), is at the right temperature, and is always ready when it is required.

Whichever feeding method is chosen by the mother, there is no set amount of sucking time within which an infant will complete a feed. Some gulp eagerly while others take it more slowly. Some infants are satisfied with a short feed, whereas others suckle for long periods at a time. Parents and carers soon learn to understand their individual infant's needs.

Weight

Within the first few days after birth infants can lose up to 10 per cent of their birth-weight, but this has usually been regained by the time they are ten days old.

The umbilicus

At birth the umbilical cord is clamped and cut, and the clamp is usually removed by day two or three as the cord stump begins to dry and shrivel up. In most cases the cord stump falls off by day seven or eight, but occasionally it takes longer.

Communication

Even newborn babies communicate. They do this through a combination of crying, body movement, and eye-to-eye contact. Some infants cry a great deal, others only when hungry or uncomfortable.

Infants will often copy the expressions of their carers, for example sticking out their tongue or making a round 'O' shape with their mouth. 'Conversation' can take place when an adult talks to an infant, leaving spaces for the baby to respond. These spaces will be filled with focused expressions and coos, followed by smiles and excited body movements after a few weeks.

Sleep

Most neonates sleep a great deal of the time, averaging six four-hourly feeds in every 24-hour period. They will occasionally sleep for a longer period of time (six to seven hours) in the night, but this is not usual.

The heel prick test (Guthrie test)

Usually on day seven infants are given the heel prick test. This is used to detect two different conditions. The first is phenylketonuria (PKU), which is a rare blood disorder, and the second is hypothyroidism, an endocrine disorder affecting how the thyroid gland functions. Both these conditions can be successfully controlled if they are detected at this early stage through the PKU test and the thyroid stimulating hormone (TSH) test respectively.

Development in general

By three or four weeks most neonates can be seen to take considerable interest in what is going on around them. They respond with their bodies to being handled, and their facial expressions include frowns, quizzical looks and intense stares. Towards the end of this first important stage in life, their limbs gradually become less flexed and infants start to settle into the family routine.

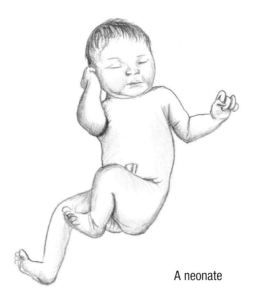

A neonate

JASMINE

Jasmine: the neonate

Jasmine followed the typical development of the neonate in most ways. She slept a great deal between feeds, with just occasional periods of wakefulness (usually at night!). Once feeding was established she suckled well, but often fell asleep during a feed and tended to feed little and often some days. By seven days old, she began to sleep for one longer stretch in each 24-hour period, but as her weight was slow to return to her birth level, her mother was advised to wake her after 4–5 hours. Feeding her when she was so sleepy was not always successful either!

On day three Jasmine copied an 'O' mouth shape, and on day four she poked out her tongue in response to an adult.

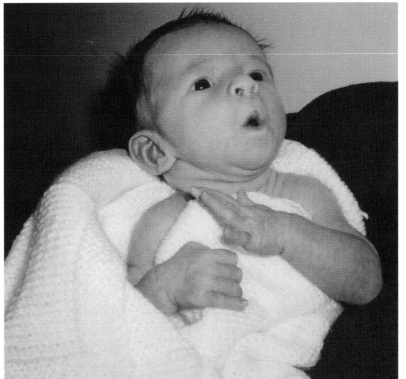

Copying carer's expression

By day eight Jasmine's eyes began to 'cross' and wander less often, but her skin became blotchy with white spots (milia). This may have been triggered by a bath preparation her mother had used, and she was advised to use only clear water for a while.

Jasmine blinked rapidly at loud noises, particularly when the family dog started barking, and she also visibly jumped on such occasions. She turned her head towards the sound of her mother's voice and clearly enjoyed being cuddled. Her hands grasped anything they touched and their strength was clearly evident when, at one hour old, she was lifted by the midwife from her mother and took a small blanket with her!

Her mouth rooted for the breast whenever she was held by her mother and she often sucked her fist. At 24 days old she found her thumb and began to suck that instead. By three weeks Jasmine was already showing great interest in the toy lion that hung over her Moses basket, staring at it intently. By week four she 'talked' to the dangling lion and to her baby gym as she lay underneath it. At this stage her weight was 3 kg (6 lb 11½ oz).

Unlike most infants, Jasmine's umbilical stump did not fall off until day 14. While there was no particular reason for this it was considered quite unusual. The heel prick test was not carried out until day eight on account of Jasmine's slow weight gain.

By two or three weeks the reduced flexion in Jasmine's limbs could be easily seen at bathtime, and by four weeks her posture was far more relaxed. Initially, Jasmine lay quite curled up in the typically flexed 'foetal' position.

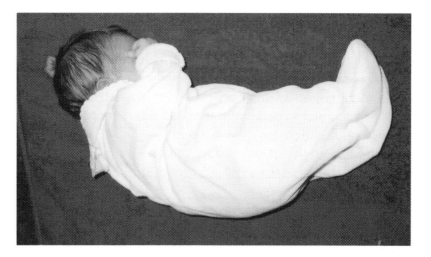

At times she was extremely active, moving from side to side, with very energetic head and limb movements.

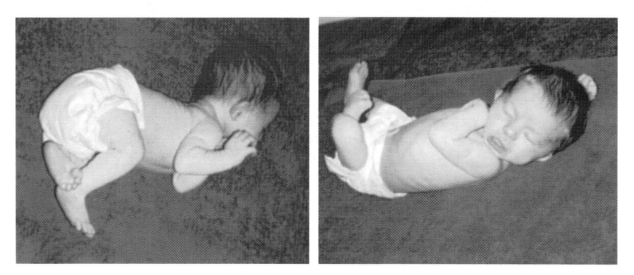

When laid prone, Jasmine struggled to lift her head, but could not manage it.

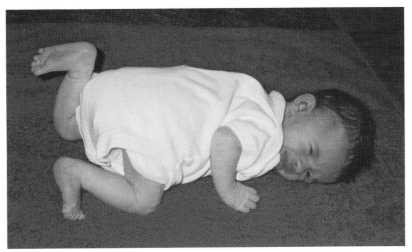

Unable to lift her head

Checkpoint questions (see Appendix at back of book for answers)

1. Describe the common features of a neonate.
2. What primitive reflexes can you explain?
3. What is vernix caseosa?
4. What is the usual cause of neonatal jaundice?
5. What does the Apgar score measure?
6. What effects can the mother's hormones passing across the placenta have on an infant?
7. Which birthmark is usually only found on dark-skinned infants?
8. Which fontanelle closes over by 18 months?
9. Infants born to black parents are usually pale at birth. Why do you think this is?
10. What factors can affect a developing foetus?
11. Why is folic acid considered to be an important supplement for pregnant women?
12. What screening processes during pregnancy can you explain?
13. What are centile charts?
14. What is the difference between the following pregnancy screening procedures: amniocentesis and chorionic villi sampling?
15. Explain the difference between a genetically inherited disorder and a congenital disorder.
16. What is the difference between genotype and phenotype?
17. How does foetal alcohol syndrome affect infants?
18. What are the most common effects of smoking in pregnancy on an infant?
19. What is the difference between the terms 'hypertonic' and 'hypotonic' when referring to the physical appearance of a newborn baby?
20. Why is Vitamin K given at birth?
21. What impact might the introduction of formula feed have had on the establishment of Jasmine's breast-feeding?
22. Where would Jasmine be placed on the centile charts at birth?
23. How much weight is considered normal for an infant to lose in the first few days?
24. What causes vaginal blood loss and swollen breasts in a neonate?

2 An introduction to general development (one month to two years)

This chapter covers children's development from one month to two years. In the sections that follow, development in general terms will be explored in relation to a number of stages within an infant's life:

- one month
- three months
- six months
- nine months
- 12 months
- 15 months
- 18 months
- two years.

Each section starts with a description of development at a given (age) stage and ends with a summary of our 'real' child (Jasmine)'s development at the same age. For example, following a general examination of development at six months, Jasmine at four, five and six months is described. This helps to demonstrate how development varies across a 'normal' range. Checkpoint questions have been interspersed in the text wherever it was felt to be relevant.

Each (age) stage is explored in relation to four key development areas:

1. Physical development – gross
2. Physical development – fine
3. Social and emotional development
4. Intellectual, sensory and language development.

Let's start by examining each of these in turn.

Physical development

Physical development falls into two main categories: it can be 'gross' (involving large actions and movements), or it can be 'fine' (precise movements and actions). Included in these categories are controlled movements and carefree movements, together with the development of balance.

Physical development involves the acquisition of locomotor skills, in which the body moves from place to place in one direction or another, for example crawling, walking or running. It also involves the acquisition of non-locomotor skills, where movement can occur while remaining in one place, for example bending forwards, pushing, pulling, or stretching up for something.

Another aspect of physical development is the increase in our range of manipulative skills. These are actions that use dexterity, such as building bricks in a tower, throwing a ball, or dressing a doll.

As development progresses it becomes a more complex process. These maturational changes include a child's ability to progress from:

- *'simple' actions towards 'complex' actions* – for example, where the child needs to be able to stand before he is able to walk.
- *'cephalo' (the head) to 'caudal' (the tail)* – for example physical development starts with the infant attaining head control initially, before being able to sit unsupported and then eventually learning how to stand and walk.
- *'proximal' (near to the body) to 'distal' (the outer reaches of the body)* – for example, toddlers can carry a large soft toy by hugging it to them, before they have the skills to fasten buttons or toggles on the toy's clothing.
- *'general' to 'specific'* – for example, a young infant uses his whole body to express himself, perhaps showing excitement at the arrival of a familiar person; whereas an older child is more likely to show pleasure through a beaming smile.

Social and emotional development

Social and emotional development refers to the way in which children develop as individuals in their own right. It is about relationships and friendships, how they learn to play and interact with others, and how they deal with and express their developing feelings, concerns, frustrations and emotions.

Babies appear to have an instinct that makes them want to interact with other human beings. This is called 'pro-social' behaviour. The range of people with whom an infant comes into contact will help build on the infant's social development. This can be through primary socialisation (the impact of the child's parents and immediate family), and through secondary socialisation (the impact of the extended family, close friends and other carers such as childminders and day nursery professionals).

Play forms an essential part of social development, and builds up through a number of stages. These stages can be divided into the following categories:

- solitary play
- parallel play
- associative (looking on) play
- simple cooperative (joining-in) play
- complex cooperative play.

For more details on these play stages see pages 141–4.

Intellectual, sensory and language development

When exploring these areas of development the principal focus is on how infants make sense of the environment into which they have been born. It is about how they explore, investigate, develop understanding, question, and express themselves.

There are many different theories about how a child's understanding develops. A brief overview of some of the central theories (with some examples) is given in Chapter 3. The theories covered are:

- assimilation and accommodation
- classical conditioning
- operant conditioning
- gender stereotyping
- object permanence
- attachment, separation and bonding
- social learning theory
- language development, including:
  - association theory
  - biological theory
  - behaviourist theory
  - maturational theory
  - interactionist theory.

In addition, Table 3.1 on page 107, sets out the stages of an infant's language development, showing the progression of sounds, words and phrases, and the infant's developing use of grammar.

Age: one month

Physical development – gross

At one month:

- legs kick and arms wave in jerky uncoordinated movements
- infants usually try to lift up their head when laid prone (on their tummy)
- head lag is seen due to undeveloped muscles in the neck
- some babies are now less 'fisted' than at birth
- infants hold their head centrally when held in ventral suspension.

Physical development – fine

At one month:

- the imitation of adult facial expressions is sometimes seen (tongue poking or making an 'O' shape with the mouth)
- infants grasp whatever they touch, e.g. a finger
- hands move in an uncontrolled way
- infants' fists may find their mouth
- facial expressions indicate pleasure.

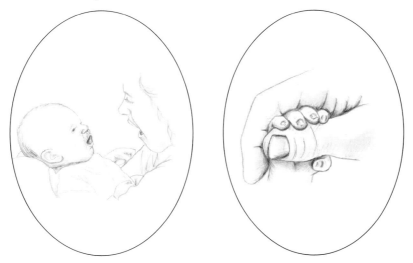

Social and emotional development

At one month:

- first signs of early smiles may be seen
- the cries of an infant are usually different depending on how the child is feeling (e.g. tired, hungry, etc.)
- cooing and gurgling noises will be made
- infants gaze at the faces of their main carers
- they turn their head in the direction of voices
- a clear enjoyment of sucking is usually evident
- babies display evidence of pleasure when being handled.

Intellectual, sensory and language development

At one month:

- infants' cries are now more expressive, making it possible to differentiate between those caused by hunger, discomfort and so on
- coos and gurgles are frequent
- infants blink if something comes towards them
- they usually 'track' the movement of a toy or a bright object dangling nearby
- imitation of adult facial expressions is sometimes seen (tongue poking or making an 'O' shape with the mouth)
- infants are usually startled by sudden noises
- the mother (or main carer) is identified by smell

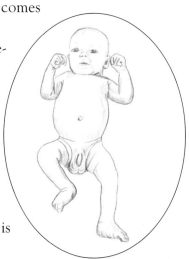
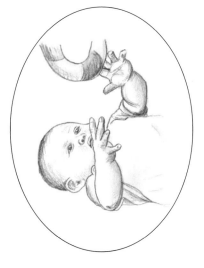

- visual focus is only around 30 cm (12 inches)
- the voice of their main carer often soothes distressed infants
- their heads turn towards sounds
- infants clearly respond when talked to, through sounds and body movements
- their eyes follow objects
- their needs are indicated through agitated movements

A summary of Jasmine's development at one month

Physical development – gross

At one month:

- there was no sign of jaundice
- she had no birthmarks
- head lag was still present
- Jasmine tried to lift her head (but not as yet successfully).

Physical development – fine

At one month:

- Jasmine reached out towards the mobile suspended above her cot
- she imitated adult facial expressions
- she grasped items with her fists (palmar grasp)
- she found her thumb at $3^{1}/_{2}$ weeks.

Jasmine found her thumb

Social and emotional development

At one month:

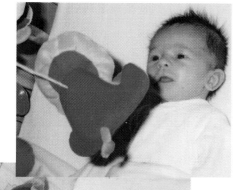

- Jasmine started to 'talk' to items on her baby gym
- her first social smiles were seen during her fourth week
- she 'cooed' at her carers
- she turned her head in response to mother's voice.

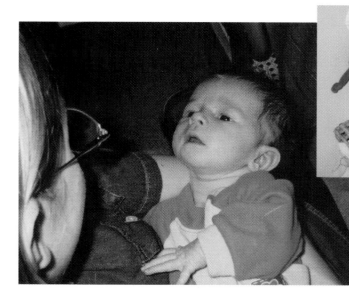

Intellectual, sensory and language development

At one month:

- Jasmine visually tracked moving objects
- she was startled easily by sudden noises
- she responded to comforting by her mother instantly
- from four to six weeks, Jasmine was very interested in objects with vertical stripes, such as folds in the curtains. These held her attention for long periods of time.

? Checkpoint questions

1. By what age is the social smile usually present?
2. What are gross motor skills?
3. What are fine motor skills?

Age: three months

Physical development – gross

At three months:

- the head can now be lifted when babies are laid prone (on their tummy)
- the head is normally kept above the body line when babies are held in ventral suspension
- there is minimal head lag seen in most infants
- with their arms held, infants will sit up straight
- legs kick vigorously, alternating between left and right, and occasionally moving together
- arms wave symmetrically
- infants can usually take their weight on their forearms when raising themselves up
- if held standing, infants sag at the knees
- movement around their cot may be considerable.

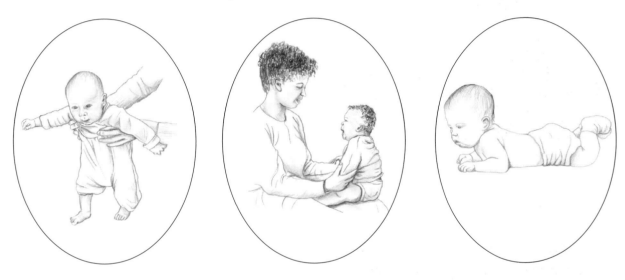

Physical development – fine

At three months:

- infants take their hands to their mouth regularly
- attempts are normally made to reach and grasp a toy, but infants have no strength as yet
- toys are grasped firmly if placed in an infant's hand
- infants play with their own fingers.

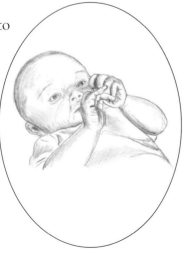

Social and emotional development

At three months:

- bathtime and caring routines are clearly enjoyed by infants
- infants stare at their carer when feeding
- a clear enjoyment of attention and being handled is shown through the infants' body movements
- many facial expressions are seen, indicating how the babies are feeling
- sudden noises still cause distress
- infants smile readily for anyone and everyone
- infants are quietened by their main carer's voice.

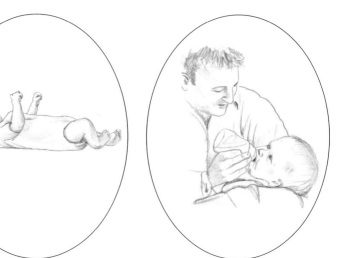

Intellectual, sensory and language development

At three months:

- the eyes now focus quite well
- infants 'turn-take' frequently with carers (i.e. they make eye contact, coo and smile in turns)
- head and eyes usually follow a moving toy through 180 degrees
- eyes often follow the movement of an adult
- infants now chuckle as well as coo and gurgle
- they continue to smile freely at everyone
- there are now more defined periods of wakefulness
- recognition of familiar music is evident
- infants are visually very alert
- much exploration takes place through the mouth
- understanding of action and effect is beginning to be seen (e.g. if an infant's foot kicks a bunny on a ribbon and the bunny moves, the infant will kick it again)

- infants cry when uncomfortable
- infants turn towards sounds and voices.

JASMINE

A summary of Jasmine's development at two months

Physical development – gross

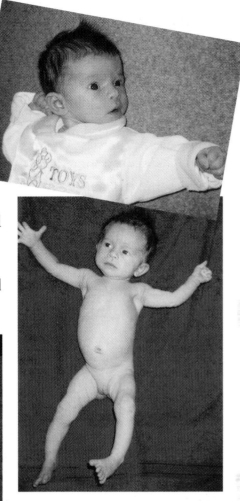

At two months:

- Jasmine waved her legs and arms excitedly at mobiles and when under the baby gym
- her limbs were constantly on the move
- her limbs had become much less flexed than previously
- Jasmine had non-symmetrical, uncoordinated, jerky movements
- when sitting, she held her head erect for several seconds before dropping it again
- her spine was less frequently curved
- when prone (on her tummy) she could hold her head up briefly

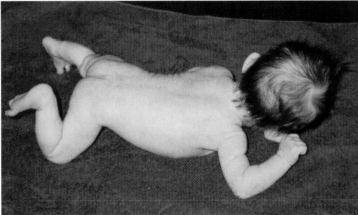

- when supine (on her back) she turned mostly to the right and appeared to almost roll over
- as her weight was still low, it was being monitored carefully by health professionals.

Physical development – fine

At two months:

- Jasmine reached for items hanging from the baby gym
- she tried to grasp a satin ribbon as it passed over her face
- at seven weeks Jasmine showed great interest in her hands. She appeared to 'wash' them in front of her eyes.

Social and emotional development

At two months:

- Jasmine watched her mobile intently
- she had her first injections at eight weeks, one jab in each thigh. Jasmine screamed and was not easily consoled. Her temperature became raised and she needed to be given paediatric paracetamol for 36 hours
- real tears were now seen when she cried
- Jasmine clearly showed enjoyment of her bath through a series of contented body movements
- breast-feeding was going extremely well.

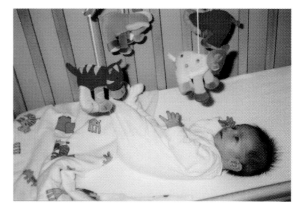

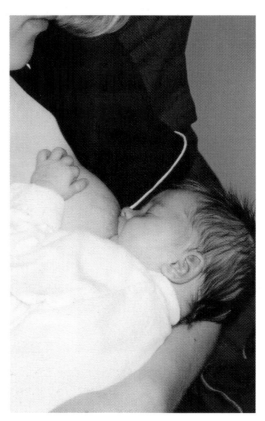

Intellectual, sensory and language development

At two months:

- Jasmine clearly listened to the musical toy on her baby gym
- she was constantly striving to look around her
- her eyes followed her mobile as it moved
- she tried to 'catch' a satin ribbon in her mouth as it was stroked over her face
- she smiled at the sensation of the satin ribbon
- she responded bodily to her own image in a mirror (but did not as yet know it was her).

? **Checkpoint questions**

1. What reasons could be given to explain Jasmine's (or any infant's) slow weight gain?
2. At what age would you expect an infant to roll over from supine to prone?
3. At what age do infants begin to show awareness rather than passive acceptance of care routines?

JASMINE

A summary of Jasmine's development at three months

Physical development – gross

At three months:

- Jasmine clearly enjoyed sitting up and looking around while in her bouncy chair
- she weighed 4.10 kg (8 lb 13½ oz), placing her on the 0.4th centile.

Physical development – fine

At three months:

- Jasmine's eyes crossed when her hands were near to her face.

Social and emotional development

At three months:

- Jasmine focused on her mother's face when feeding
- she was sleeping regularly for six hours each night
- she was awake much more during the day
- she was very alert to what was going on around her
- Jasmine enjoyed a massage
- she chuckled, cooed and gurgled, turn-taking with adults
- by nine weeks she had social smiles for everyone
- Jasmine had her second dose of triple injections. This time her mother gave her paediatric paracetamol beforehand and her temperature remained normal
- she was visibly calmed by various types of music, including Pachelbel's Canon and anything by the musical artist Sinead O'Connor, and by her mother's voice
- she showed real enjoyment of her bath
- by ten weeks Jasmine slept regularly for seven hours a night

Intellectual, sensory and language development

At three months:

- Jasmine enjoyed kicking her feet on the piano keys and repeated the action to hear the sound again
- she continued to 'wash' her hands in front of her face
- at ten weeks Jasmine copied a 'hand grasp' action.

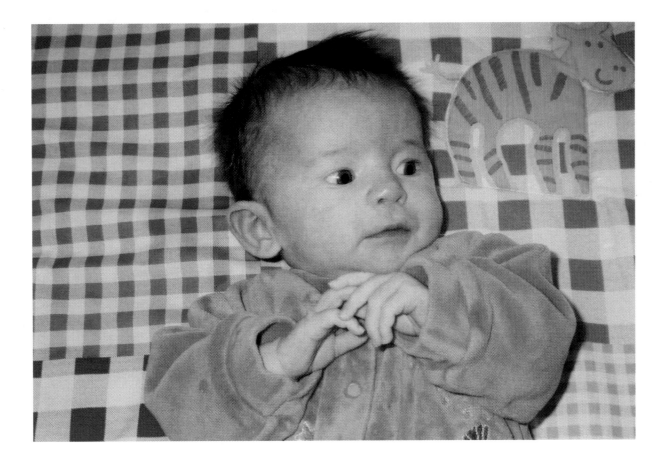

? Checkpoint questions

1. Why do babies enjoy a massage?
2. What does the triple vaccine protect against?
3. What does the HiB vaccine protect against?

Age: six months

Physical development – gross

At six months:

- infants can normally now roll from supine (on their back) to prone (on their tummy)
- rolling from prone to supine position is occasionally seen, but usually takes a little longer
- if holding an adult's fingers, infants can usually pull themselves up into a sitting position
- they may be able to sit unsupported for a brief time
- head control has now been attained
- when prone, infants start to draw up their knees ready for crawling at a later date
- some infants will 'commando' crawl (on their tummies, using their arms to move themselves along)
- when held standing, infants like to bounce on their feet, but their legs can rarely take all their weight
- infants grasp their own feet when supine
- kicking is energetic, and legs move alternately
- arms may be held up by those infants wanting to be lifted.

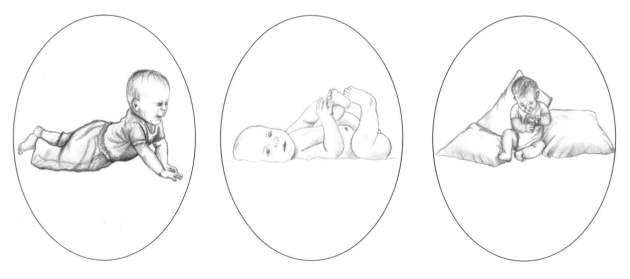

Physical development – fine

At six months:

- infants reach for a rattle or a toy, and deliberately shake it
- infants usually become very interested in their own feet
- they watch a toy when their grasp has released it accidently
- toys are grasped with the whole hand (palmar grasp)
- they will occasionally be passed from hand to hand
- infants often grab the spoon when feeding
- both hands are normally used to reach and grasp a toy (the 'two-handed' scoop)
- the index finger is used by infants to poke objects that are of interest to them.

Social and emotional development

At six months:

- infants pat the breast or bottle contentedly when feeding
- most are still happy to be near strangers, but some babies show signs of wariness
- infants clearly enjoy the company of others
- they may start to hold finger foods
- they may get distressed if the main carer leaves.

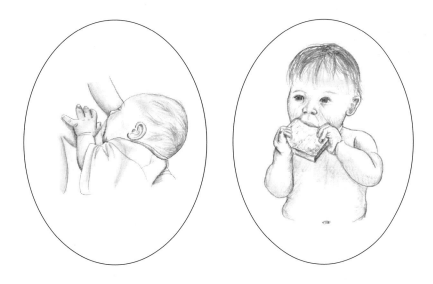

Intellectual, sensory and language development

At six months:

- infants immediately turn towards the sound of their main carer's voice
- they take everything to their mouth
- visually they are insatiable, their head and eyes moving constantly
- desires are made known through sounds and body language

- they now laugh, chuckle and squeal out loud
- infants will sometimes scream in annoyance or frustration
- vocalisations are quite tuneful (e.g. 'erlahlah', 'mamama' and so on)
- familiar sounds often stop infants crying
- they will sometimes imitate sounds.

A summary of Jasmine's development at four months

Physical development – gross

At four months:

- Jasmine's weight was 4.592 kg (10 lb 2 oz). This now took her to just below the 0.4th centile on the growth charts
- when supine, Jasmine banged her feet up and down. She was clearly amused by this achievement
- Jasmine now enjoyed sitting propped up with cushions
- she was happier now on her tummy, as she had more strength in her arms and could push herself up.

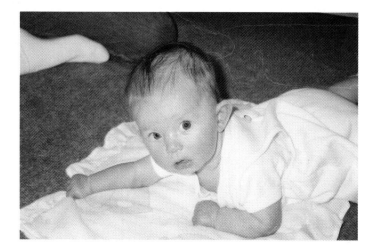

Physical development – fine

At four months:

- if offered a rattle, Jasmine held it firmly and rattled it vigorously
- she had limited control over her fine movements and needed constant supervision to ensure she did not hit herself with toys and rattles
- when introduced to solids Jasmine soon managed to coordinate her mouth and tongue to take them
- she was offered a cup of water, but could not as yet manage to drink any of it
- Jasmine refused to suck a bottle.

Social and emotional development

At four months:

- Jasmine slept between 9 and 10 hours at night, waking once for a quick breast-feed
- she started to have solids, including rice (made initially with formula), potato and gravy (gluten-free), and stewed apple
- she smiled at anyone who gave her attention
- she smiled at the family pets as they moved past her.

Intellectual, sensory and language development

At four months:

- Jasmine looked around her with interest when she was sat up
- she clearly listened intensely to household noises
- she was fascinated by mobiles and their constant motion, showing her excitement through jerky body movements
- she responded to anything dangly
- Jasmine responded with face and body to tactile experiences (e.g. satin ribbons, silk scarves, etc.)
- she rooted for items whenever they passed her face or mouth
- she chuckled and cooed conversationally with familiar adults.

? Checkpoint questions

1. What steps might be taken if an infant's weight does not begin to increase?
2. Why are solid foods introduced between four and six months?
3. Why is it recommended that infants are given gluten-free foods for the first few months?
4. What precautions should be taken regarding pets when there is an infant around?

JASMINE

A summary of Jasmine's development at five months

Physical development – gross

At five months:

- Jasmine could turn 360 degrees when on her back
- at 20 weeks she sat briefly without support
- she could now roll from her tummy to her back (prone to supine)
- Jasmine could suck her big toes!
- Her weight was now 5.528 kg (12 lb 3 oz), which took her almost to the second centile on her growth chart.

Physical development – fine

At five months:

- Jasmine could catch her feet with her hands
- she liked to hold her knees when they were bare, caressing and smoothing them
- she could now grab the items hanging from her baby gym and move them along unaided
- she tried to grab the spoon when being fed
- Jasmine grabbed her cup of water and chewed the spout (but still could not suck it)
- she pulled her lion onto her tummy when laid supine
- she learned to splash her hands in the water at bathtime.

Social and emotional development

At five months:

- Jasmine had her third triple injection (at 19 weeks). Again she was given paracetamol beforehand to ensure that her temperature stayed down
- she still enjoyed having solids, to which had been added banana, and rice with stewed pear.

Intellectual, sensory and language development

At five months:

- Jasmine vocalised loudly, clearly enjoying the sound of her own voice
- she screeched, laughed and spluttered
- Jasmine continued to turn-take with familiar adults
- she copied Mummy's voice – making 'two-syllable' sounds
- she laughed out loud, especially if tickled
- she started to suck in her lips in response to adults' actions
- she laughed at Granny singing!
- Jasmine had a pseudo (false) squint. She has quite a wide bridge to her nose, which sometimes gives this appearance. To ascertain whether a squint is a 'real squint' or a 'pseudo squint', you need to look at the baby when a bright object is being reflected in his eyes. If you can (simultaneously) see the reflected object in the same place in both of the baby's eyes, the squint is 'pseudo' as opposed to 'real'.

A summary of Jasmine's development at six months

Physical development – gross

At six months:

- Jasmine was now very strong when laid prone, holding herself up well on her arms
- Jasmine moved backwards when prone and occasionally moved round in circles (this was done very subtly so that you were not always aware that she was moving)
- the first signs of teething were being seen – dribbling and chewing hard
- Jasmine sat more securely now, but still needed support most of the time
- Jasmine now started to go swimming each week and loved the freedom it gave her to move and splash in the water
- she became much more active at bathtime, probably as a result of going swimming.

Physical development – fine

At six months:

- Jasmine now passed toys from hand to hand
- she sat in her highchair and held onto the sides of the tray
- the pincer grasp (where small objects are held between index finger and thumb) was clearly developing
- Jasmine could now drink a little water from a cup.

Social and emotional development

At six months:

- Jasmine sat in a highchair for her meals
- she continued to be very sociable, enjoying the company of other people.

Intellectual, sensory and language development

At six months:

- Jasmine made the sounds 'mum mum mum' and 'yi yi yi'
- she 'sucked' her lips (lip smacking) in response to adult kisses, finding the sensation very funny.

 **Checkpoint questions**

1. Jasmine's health visitor says she has a pseudo squint. What is this?
2. What foods are suitable to offer a six-month-old infant?
3. What stimulating activities would you provide for an infant of around six months?

Age: nine months

Physical development – gross

At nine months:

- infants can now move between positions (e.g. from sitting to crawling, or crawling to sitting)
- they usually sit up or roll over to get off their back
- they can usually pull themselves up to a standing position, but cannot as yet lower themselves back down again
- when standing, infants lean their body against furniture or other solid objects and take their weight on their feet
- most infants crawl or bottom shuffle
- interest is often shown in climbing the stairs
- infants are very active physically
- infants usually sit well unsupported
- a step may be taken if both hands are held.

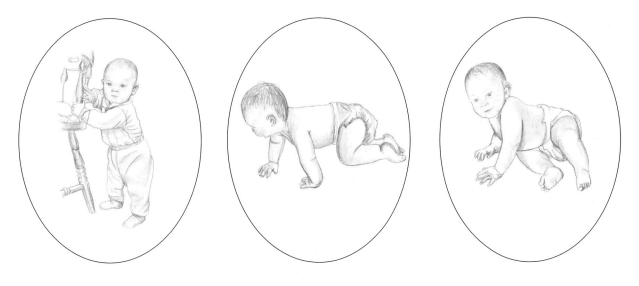

Physical development – fine

At nine months:

- infants put their hands around the breast or bottle during a milk feed
- they try to grasp the spoon at mealtimes
- infants comfortably hold finger foods. They bite, chew and feed themselves small items such as raisins
- hands are now put together on purpose
- toys are held out to adults for them to take

- infants pass toys from hand to hand
- the pincer grasp is emerging (using the index finger and thumb to pick things up with)
- arms move excitedly in pleasure
- infants point to items they want.

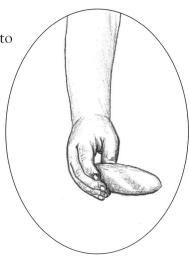

Social and emotional development

At nine months:

- infants are now clearly interested in other infants
- small lumps of food are now chewed quite well at mealtimes
- infants enjoy playing games such as 'Peekabo'
- they are less happy with strangers, often showing great wariness and needing reassurance if their main carer leaves
- infants often throw back their body and stiffen in protest (e.g. when being positioned in their pushchair)
- infants often become distressed if other infants are crying
- they watch the activity of others with great interest.

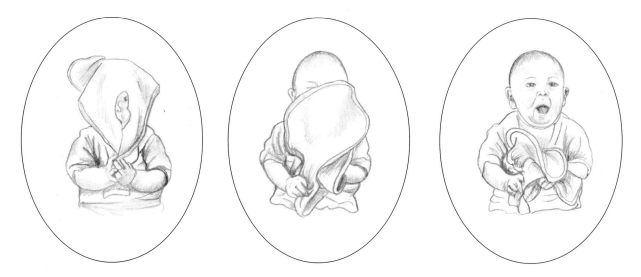

Intellectual, sensory and language development

At nine months:

- infants' attention spans are gradually increasing
- infants investigate toys and objects for long periods (a characteristic identified by the psychologist Jean Piaget, who called this the 'sensory motor stage')
- everything is still taken to the mouth
- infants can find a toy that has been partly hidden (object permanence)
- they usually understand the words 'no' and 'bye bye'
- the activities of others are watched with great interest
- toys that they have dropped are now looked for by infants
- infants babble tunefully
- they usually copy sounds such as a cough or a 'raspberry'
- vocalisations are used deliberately to communicate with others
- actions are repeated if they gain a positive response from the adult.

A summary of Jasmine's development at seven months

Physical development – gross

At seven months:

- Jasmine was moving all round the floor, but was not yet actually crawling. She mostly moved backwards and sideways, using her whole body in the process
- when laid prone, Jasmine's legs moved forwards, but her hands remained still so that her bottom rose higher and higher until eventually she toppled over
- Jasmine moved into the family bath, where she had much more room to splash around and be active.

Physical development – fine

At seven months:

- Jasmine was very skilful at feeding herself finger foods (rice cakes, toast, and slivers of banana)
- her pincer grasp was now very good; she picked up tiny fibres from the carpet and daisies and grass when in the garden
- Jasmine reached for toys on the floor and other items that interested her
- from 6½ months Jasmine began to hold finger foods, such as baby rice cakes.

Social and emotional development

At seven months:

- Jasmine now showed a definite recognition of many family members and greeted everyone with huge smiles, throwing herself backwards in excitement.

Intellectual, sensory and language development

At seven months:

- Jasmine was clearly fascinated by the family pets
- she tried to grab the cats as they passed by (careful supervision was needed)
- when out in her pushchair Jasmine was fascinated by pigeons
- she was very interested in photographs of herself
- she was very interested in pictures of babies, but remained passive when shown pictures of people in general
- Jasmine stared, and watched 'life' intently
- she was very loud vocally, still mostly saying 'mum mum mum' and 'yi yi yi'
- she sucked bath water from her bath sponge, clearly delighted with the experience!

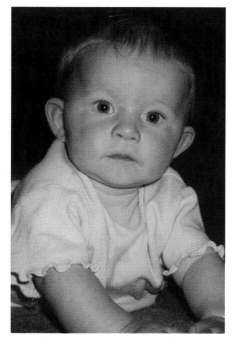

? Checkpoint questions

1. From what age can babies be taken swimming?
2. Why do babies move backwards in the earliest stages of mobility?
3. Does hand preference at this age give an accurate indication for the future?
4. Why might Jasmine particularly respond to pictures of babies?
5. What finger foods are ideal to first offer babies?
6. From what age would you expect a baby to crawl?

Physical development – gross

At eight months:

- Jasmine had her eight-month paediatric check-up and all was well.

- Jasmine had become very mobile, crawling in the traditional manner and also starting to 'bear-walk' (moving using her hands and feet)

- Jasmine had also begun to sit up from crawling

- her weight was now 6.69 kg (14 lb 12½ oz), just above the second centile on her growth chart. Although clearly very light for her age, health professionals were not concerned, as Jasmine was bright, content and very active!

Physical development – fine

At eight months:

- Jasmine preferred finger foods to being fed with a spoon
- she used her whole hand to pat the items in which she had a particular interest, such as pictures in books.

Social and emotional development

At eight months:

- Jasmine showed a definite preference for eating finger foods
- her parents responded by giving her meals consisting of 'soft' pieces of food
- she could now drink water well from a feeder beaker
- she always smiled at her favoured toys.

Intellectual, sensory and language development

At eight months:

- Jasmine was very vocal, using a diverse range of sounds and pitches
- she clearly loved to hear herself squeal
- her main sounds included 'mamama', 'bababa' and 'ayoh'
- she showed great interest in picture books, patting the pages with pleasure
- Jasmine returned to her favourite toys (her teething bunny and a dog that barks) over and over again.

 Checkpoint questions

1. At what age would you usually replace an infant's milk feed with water as an accompaniment to meals?
2. As a baby becomes more mobile, what safety precautions would you need to take?

JASMINE

A summary of Jasmine's development at nine months

Physical development – gross

At nine months:

- Jasmine could pull herself up into a standing position using a piece of furniture for support
- she could move sideways along solid items such as the sofa.

Physical development – fine

At nine months:

- Jasmine manipulated all objects with increasing dexterity
- she had an extremely well-developed pincer grasp
- she handled the items in her treasure basket (a small basket filled with safe and stimulating 'natural' objects) carefully and with interest (see pages 145–6 for more on treasure baskets)
- Jasmine tried to hold the spoon when being fed, but still preferred to use her hands.

Social and emotional development

At nine months:

- Jasmine chewed well at mealtimes
- she enjoyed an increasingly varied range of foods
- she still preferred to feed herself with her hands
- Jasmine loved the attention given to her by other people
- she loved to be chased when she crawled
- she was beginning to enjoy playing 'Peekabo' with others.

Intellectual, sensory and language development

At nine months:

- Jasmine could now find toys that had been partially hidden (she had acquired object permanence)
- she was fascinated by her own reflection in a full-length mirror, looking behind it to 'find' the baby who was facing her
- she loved exploring her treasure basket, concentrating hard on each object in turn
- she used hands and mouth to 'sense' each item in her treasure basket
- she 'listened' to a large shell, imitating what she had been shown to do
- she also put her ear to large beakers and other similar objects
- Jasmine was beginning to show real excitement when playing games such as 'Peekabo'.

? Checkpoint questions

1. Jasmine's mother prepared her a treasure basket. What items might you find in this?
2. Jasmine has an established 'pincer grasp'. What is this?
3. What is the term used to describe an infant's understanding that an object exists even when it cannot be seen?

Age: 12 months

Physical development – gross

At 12 months:

- infants now sit well, and for long periods of time
- they can pull themselves to standing and lower themselves down again
- infants side-step around the furniture
- if one or both hands are held, infants will usually walk
- they may stand unaided for short periods of time
- some infants will be able to crawl upstairs
- infants are less likely to lean against furniture for balance
- some infants will move around using their hands and feet (bear-walking).

Physical development – fine

At 12 months:

- a neat pincer grasp (between index finger and thumb) is usual
- infants drop and throw toys and objects, and watch them fall
- both hands are used freely, but hand preference may be shown
- infants point and poke with their index finger
- they can now release a small toy or object into an adult's hand
- activities such as shape sorters are enjoyed

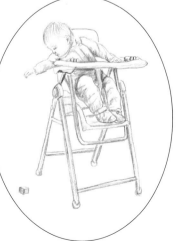

- infants try to turn the pages of a book
- building a tower of two bricks may be achieved
- most infants will clap.

Social and emotional development

At 12 months:

- infants can usually drink from a cup with some assistance
- they usually hold out an arm to help when dressing
- most infants wave on request, and sometimes spontaneously too
- infants enjoy playing 'Pat-a-cake'
- they have fun playing with an adult
- most infants are very affectionate
- they like to be within sight and hearing of familiar adults.

Intellectual, sensory and language development

At 12 months:

- toys are taken to the mouth less often
- infants can quickly find a toy that they have seen hidden
- actions that have produced a sound are usually repeated
- imitation is seen (e.g. rattling a spoon in a cup)
- infants know their own name and respond to it
- they vocalise loudly and incessantly, using jargon in a 'conversational' manner
- intonation of the voice is developing
- infants' behaviour shows an understanding of many words, including 'come to Daddy', 'wave bye bye' and so on

- recognition of familiar sounds and voices is evident
- infants respond to requests such as 'come here', 'clap hands' and so on
- they now point when looking at something specific
- one word (sometimes two) is usual for the age, commonly a noun (e.g. 'duck').

A summary of Jasmine's development at ten months

Physical development – gross

At ten months:

- Jasmine had her first four teeth – central incisors – which arrived with no real problems
- she also learned to grind her teeth together!
- Jasmine was increasingly agile in moving around the furniture and floor.

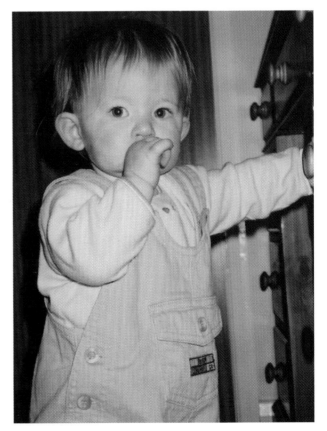

Physical development – fine

At ten months:

- Jasmine's hands and fingers quivered and flexed in excited anticipation as she went to touch surfaces that particularly gave her pleasure, especially the family dog and cats
- she explored every surface that she came across.

Social and emotional development

At ten months:

- Jasmine could now blows kisses to close family members
- she loved a cuddle
- she was able to be apart from her parents for short periods of time (looked after by Granny), but showed great delight on seeing them return
- Jasmine had not as yet shown any great wariness of strangers, but the current living arrangements meant that there was always a familiar adult around.

Intellectual, sensory and language development

At ten months:

- Jasmine understood the words 'no' and 'don't touch', shown by her shaking her head as she reached out to touch objects that she knew were off limits (e.g. flowers, plants, books, etc.)
- Jasmine looked to see if she was being watched as she hesitated prior to touching something she shouldn't
- she played contentedly alone
- Jasmine could build a tower of two bricks with increasing success
- she showed a definite preference for anything that was yellow.

? Checkpoint questions

1. At what age would you expect an infant to wave?
2. In which order do teeth usually appear?

A summary of Jasmine's development at 11 months

Physical development – gross

At 11 months:

- Jasmine's movements round the furniture were getting quicker and quicker
- she could neatly side-step as she moved, keeping her balance even if she stumbled over toys
- Jasmine could occasionally stand for brief moments without support, concentrating on an item in her hand, or while she had a drink
- she could let herself down to the floor with a degree of control, only occasionally bumping down abruptly.

Physical development – fine

At 11 months:

- Jasmine held her arms out to be lifted up, both for comfort and as a new action
- when sitting, Jasmine twisted her wrists round and round
- she could clap, patting the back of one hand with the other
- she often called her own version of 'hooray' as she clapped.

Social and emotional development

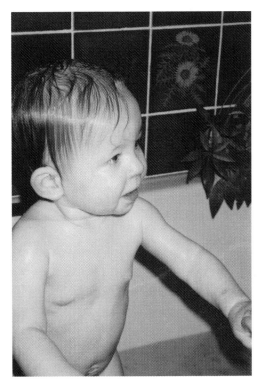

At 11 months:

- when in her highchair Jasmine often put one foot onto her tray, grinning at her parents and waiting to be asked to remove it!
- Jasmine loved bathtime.

Intellectual, sensory and language development

At 11 months:

- Jasmine would say 'duck' at the sight of anything that was yellow and resembled a bird (like her bath toy)
- she said 'ga da' (Grandad)
- she said 'dor' (dog) when Charlie, the family Labrador, was nearby
- Jasmine's family reinforced all her language attempts, resulting in her repeating them often
- she looked at each family member in turn as their name was said, showing her understanding of who was who
- Jasmine sometimes called 'hooray' when clapping
- she loved to explore all aspects of her toys in turn.

? Checkpoint questions

1. At what age would you expect an infant to be walking?
2. At what age do infants often become wary of strangers?
3. What term is used to describe the positive responses given to Jasmine by her family?

Physical development – gross

At 12 months:

- Jasmine's balance was much better
- she stood for long periods of time
- she sometimes bent down to pick things up, retaining her balance
- Jasmine's first steps were taken aged 11 months and 1 week, from her mum to her activity table
- when encouraged to walk, Jasmine got so excited that her eagerness tipped her off balance
- she could now climb onto the bottom stair
- she used a large cardboard box as a tunnel, clearly loving the freedom and the action
- her weight at one year old was 7.638 kg (16 lb 15 oz).

Physical development – fine

At 12 months:

- Jasmine 'waved bye bye', but often only after the person had gone
- she explored texture and properties of everything she came into contact with
- she dropped items from her highchair and watched them fall to the floor.

Exploring textures

Social and emotional development

At 12 months:

- Jasmine 'waved bye bye'
- she was very wary of the rocking horse she received for Christmas
- there were no real interactions seen between Jasmine and her friends at her birthday party.

Intellectual, sensory and language development

At 12 months:

- Jasmine developed her own 'question' incorporating the words 'in-air?', which is roughly translated as 'What's in there?', 'Who's in there?' or 'What's that?'
- Jasmine linked her 'question' to pictures and photographs, and to objects of particular interest to her (e.g. mirrors and the fruit bowl)
- she sorted objects from container to container
- she still took many objects to her mouth
- Jasmine loved the gift tags and 'springy' gift decorations on her presents at Christmas
- she loved touching the baubles and branches of the Christmas tree.

? Checkpoint questions

1. Jasmine has never sat in a baby-walker. Do you think that devices such as this would have helped her to walk earlier?
2. As Jasmine begins to gain confidence and takes more steps, what toys or activities will be suitable for her?
3. What new dietary options will be available to Jasmine as she reaches her first birthday?
4. What level of social behaviour would you expect to see in Jasmine at one year old?

Age: 15 months

Physical development – gross

At 15 months:

- infants usually walk alone, with uneven steps
- they often hold their arms up high to maintain balance when walking, and have their feet wide apart
- infants can start walking, but can only stop when they bump into an object or person
- they may still let themselves down to a sitting position with a bump
- infants can usually get to their feet by themselves without help
- they can usually creep upstairs well, but always need supervision
- infants can sometimes creep downstairs too (backwards)
- infants are often seen kneeling as they play
- infants enjoy pushing large wheeled toys around.

Physical development – fine

At 15 months:

- an increasing ability to manipulate toys and objects is seen
- the ability to release objects purposefully is developing
- infants point at objects that interest them
- they usually show a hand preference
- the pincer grasp is developing.

Social and emotional development

At 15 months:

- infants will try to help when they are being dressed
- they may indicate when they have a wet or soiled nappy
- constant supervision is needed to protect infants from the dangers of their own explorations
- infants try hard to feed themselves
- toys are often thrown to the floor in frustration.

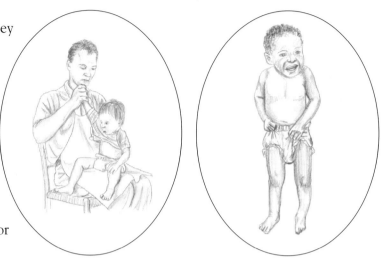

Intellectual, sensory and language development

At 15 months:

- infants are now very interested in books, songs and rhymes
- they are fascinated by all that is going on around them
- they explore all properties and possibilities of toys
- infants are intensely curious
- they particularly enjoy toys that need fitting together
- they enjoy putting things in containers
- up to six words are usually spoken, most of which are recognisable
- infants' actions show that they understand a great deal of what is going on around them
- infants jabber loudly all the time
- understanding of familiar pictures and body parts is shown by pointing.

JASMINE

A summary of Jasmine's development at 13 months

Physical development – gross

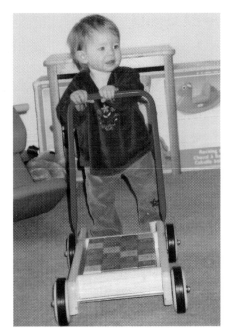

At 13 months:

- Jasmine pushed her trolley of bricks along, using it to help her balance as she walked. She could only stop by crashing into something
- more 'occasional' steps were taken every day
- Jasmine appeared to walk on the spot at times.

Physical development – fine

At 13 months:

- Jasmine liked her shape sorter toy, and handled the shapes well, successfully 'posting' many of them through the relevant holes
- she explored the clothing of her soft-bodied doll carefully, using increasing dexterity.

Social and emotional development

At 13 months:

- Jasmine put soft toys under her chin and 'loved' them, saying 'ahhh'
- she followed her playmates (Maisie and Francesca) through her cardboard tunnel – a very early shared play experience.

Intellectual, sensory and language development

At 13 months:

- Jasmine could match her soft toy cat to a similar cat in her picture book and on a puzzle. This was evidenced by her selecting them all together
- she would sometimes say 'ba' (bye) when she waved
- she spent long periods of time filling and emptying containers
- she explored the fastenings on her soft-bodied doll's clothing (e.g. zip, buttons, Velcro, etc.)
- on one occasion she could not get a shape to fit in her shape sorter so she put in through the hole in a tissue box!

? Checkpoint questions

1. What skills are being developed through the use of shape sorter toys?
2. From what age would you expect infants to be interested in books?

A summary of Jasmine's development at 14 months

Physical development – gross

At 14 months:

- Jasmine walked best when on a firm surface
- she was very unsure when walking on grass
- she clearly enjoyed the freedom of being able to walk, but sometimes still reverted to crawling (she clearly found it quicker)
- Jasmine was teething constantly, with lots of dribbling and occasional periods of distress
- by 13½ months Jasmine was walking more confidently every day, holding up her arms for balance.

Physical development – fine

At 14 months:

- Jasmine used precise manipulation to select foods and toys
- she pointed to items that interested her.

Social and emotional development

At 14 months:

- when taken to feed the ducks, Jasmine preferred to eat the bread herself
- bananas were clearly her favourite food. She often ate three a day (one at each meal)
- she loved fruit and cheese
- she enjoyed her meals
- Jasmine confidently moved away from her mum at toddler groups
- she drank more cow's milk
- she still had a breast-feed at night
- Jasmine went off to sleep well, and most nights she played for a while in her cot before settling herself to sleep
- she slept well despite teething, usually sleeping for 12–13 hours
- Jasmine loved to hide (and be found).

Intellectual, sensory and language development

At 14 months:

- Jasmine was very interested in ducks at the park and along the river
- she was fascinated by ducks walking towards her
- when offered a selection of fruit at mealtimes, she showed understanding of what they were (grapes, banana, pear, orange) by selecting the one that was named for her (i.e. when asked 'Would you like a grape, Jasmine?')
- Jasmine's most frequent word was 'nana', used for banana and also for anything else she was asking for.

❓ Checkpoint questions

1. How would you expect social play to develop at this age?
2. Jasmine ate a great deal of fruit. What aspects of a healthy diet does this contribute to?
3. What foods would complement fruit to complete a balanced diet in a toddler of Jasmine's age?
4. How can the effects of teething be relieved?

JASMINE

A summary of Jasmine's development at 15 months

Physical development – gross

At 15 months:

- Jasmine enjoyed stomping her feet in her recently bought shoes
- she liked to undress herself
- she removed her pyjamas as soon as she woke up
- on occasions Jasmine removed her nappy too!
- Jasmine used her arms for balance less often when walking
- she could climb steps quite well and was increasingly confident in getting down them again
- she tried to ride her tricycle.

Physical development – fine

At 15 months:

● Jasmine concentrated as she undressed her doll (with increasing skill), tickling his tummy with her fingers

● she picked up daisies and leaves in the garden

● she could position items carefully where she wanted them to be.

Social and emotional development

At 15 months:

● Jasmine loved to visit familiar adults (grandparents and close friends)

● she had her MMR (Measles, Mumps and Rubella) injections. Jasmine was now completely up to date with the recommended immunisation programme for the UK

● Jasmine was great friends with 'Shadow', one of the family pets (a black cat).

Jasmine and shadow were great friends

Intellectual, sensory and language development

At 15 months:

- Jasmine clearly listened to the sound of her shoes
- she concentrated hard as she undressed herself, and her doll
- she liked to pick up leaves and daisies in the garden, looking at them very carefully

- Jasmine touched flowers very gently
- she placed her nose to flowers, as shown, but could not as yet sniff
- an ever increasing understanding of her world was seen. (When sat in her pushchair, for example, Jasmine had a safety strap to hold her cup or a toy. She regularly positioned the strap over her cup or toy, waiting for an adult to secure it.)

? Checkpoint questions

1. Which areas of development is Jasmine demonstrating when she positions her safety strap in her pushchair?
2. Why is it important to have a child's shoes fitted properly?
3. What have been the main concerns regarding the MMR immunisation?
4. How might Jasmine's interest in the family pets help her development?

Age: 18 months

Physical development – gross

At 18 months:

- toddlers usually walk well, starting and stopping safely
- despite being able to run quite well, they are not yet able to avoid obstacles
- toddlers no longer need arms extended to help them balance
- pushing and pulling large toys, boxes and so on is enjoyed
- toddlers will back into a small chair to sit down
- they climb forward into an adult chair and turn round to sit
- they walk upstairs with a 'hand', both feet to each stair
- some can walk downstairs too
- toddlers frequently creep downstairs backwards on knees, or bump down on their bottom
- they often squat down to pick up toys
- hands are usually used to stand up from squatting.

Physical development – fine

At 18 months:

- toddlers can turn pages of a book quite well
- they hold a pencil in a primitive 'tripod' grip
- they can usually build 3 or more bricks into a tower
- very small items are picked up in pincer grasp (using index finger and thumb)
- toddlers can usually use a spoon successfully to feed themselves

- increasing wrist control when manipulating items is seen
- toddlers enjoy turning containers upside down to empty them
- they clap hands often.

Social and emotional development

At 18 months:

- bowel control is sometimes attained
- signs of urgency with regard to bladder and bowel movements are usually seen
- toddlers can use a spoon successfully to feed themselves
- toddlers lift cups, but usually prefer to hand them over to an adult rather than put them down
- they can take off shoes, socks and hats, but cannot replace them
- toddlers clap hands
- they are still very dependent on adults, especially their main carer
- toddlers often alternate between 'clinging' and resistance
- objects are still thrown to the floor in frustration, but less often now, and toddlers of this age seldom look for them
- they play contentedly alone, but like to be near to an adult.

Intellectual, sensory and language development

At 18 months:

- toddlers talk to themselves continuously in play
- a vocabulary of 6–20 recognisable words is usual, but they clearly understand many more
- toddlers often echo the last word said to them, or a prominent word (known as 'echolalia')
- urgent vocalisations are made when issuing a demand
- they no longer take toys to their mouth
- toddlers remember where objects belong
- they still particularly enjoy putting objects into containers
- they briefly imitate simple everyday activities (e.g. feeding a baby, reading a book, brushing hair)
- toddlers play contentedly alone
- an increased concentration span is evident

- toddlers obey simple commands (e.g. 'Fetch your shoes please')
- they remember where they left a favourite toy
- they enjoy picture books
- they recognise themselves in a mirror
- toddlers show recognition when familiar people approach them
- over-extension of word use is common (e.g. 'dog' may be used for all animals)
- most toddlers now refer to themselves by name.

A summary of Jasmine's development at 16 months

Physical development – gross

At 16 months:

- Jasmine could run confidently, and enjoyed chasing the family cats
- she could stop and start running without stumbling
- she attended a soft play centre, which she loved, running confidently, climbing through tunnels, pushing through poles and walking over netting walkways (she liked to hold a hand for this)
- Jasmine also liked the big slide at the soft play centre
- she now loved her rocking horse at home, often riding it backwards and also without holding on
- she could climb on and off furniture at home such as the sofa and chairs, and enjoyed leaping onto large beanbags.

Physical development – fine

At 16 months:

- Jasmine could carry items carefully without spilling the contents (e.g. the container of cat food to feed Granny's cats)
- she could help tip the food into the cat's bowl, but needed help to maintain control
- having recently learned how to blow, she tried hard to blow mobiles and other 'hanging' items
- she tried hard to put on her socks, but could not as yet manage it.

At 16 months:

- Jasmine liked to put things away
- she tidied up the balls that had been thrown out of the ball pool at the soft play centre
- she laughed with pleasure as she played, and expressed delight at any new achievements she made
- she tried to cuddle 'Shadow' the cat!

Intellectual, sensory and language development

At 16 months:

- Jasmine liked to dip her hands in the cats' water bowl (she needed constant supervision)
- she could 'position' her socks on top of her feet, showing a clear understanding of where they went.

? Checkpoint questions

1. Why is supervision so important in activity areas such as the soft play centre?
2. How might attending the soft play centre have contributed to Jasmine's physical development?

A summary of Jasmine's development at 17 months

Physical development – gross

At 17 months:

- Jasmine was often seen climbing steps, both feet to each step, always holding on securely
- Jasmine loved the freedom to run around in safe open spaces (e.g. the park, the zoo)
- she tried to kick a football, but fell into it
- she could climb the steps on her slide at home, one foot to each step.

Physical development – fine

At 17 months:

- when getting dressed, Jasmine was very interested in where all her items of clothing needed to go, and could indicate by pointing but could not actually put them on
- she pointed accurately at animals seen at the zoo, even the very small ones
- she particularly enjoyed opening up cardboard boxes (cereal packets etc.).

Social and emotional development

At 17 months:

- Jasmine tried to drink from a cup without a lid (with 'some' success)
- she enjoyed sharing an ice lolly with Mummy at the zoo
- she showed confidence in moving away from family members at the zoo when something of interest caught her eye
- Jasmine played contentedly alone, but liked to know where a familiar adult was at all times
- she briefly played alongside another (older) child with a football at the zoo.

Intellectual, sensory and language development

At 17 months:

- Jasmine vocalised constantly to herself in play
- she regularly made a new 'sound' – 'gollygollygollygolly' – which she always said four times. It appeared to have no meaning at all, but saying it clearly gave Jasmine a great deal of pleasure
- other recognisable words now included 'duck' (used for all birds and waterfowl) and 'car'
- Jasmine 'positioned' clothing on the correct parts of her body (e.g. trousers on top of legs, hat on her head, etc.)
- she enjoyed her visit to the zoo, focusing intently on the various animals

- she was able to visually track the animals at the zoo remarkably easily, even quite small ones
- she showed a particular fascination for turtles, geckos and iguanas
- Jasmine loved the fish in the underwater world, but drew back in surprise as a shark swam (directly) towards her
- all birds at the zoo were 'ducks' to Jasmine (over-extension of word use)
- Jasmine frowned at the coldness of her ice lolly as she sucked it, and seemed surprised at how cold it felt to her fingers when she touched it.

? Checkpoint questions

1. Jasmine referred to all birds as ducks, a usual stage in a toddler's development. Why is this do you think?
2. Why might Jasmine have shrunk back from the shark in the underwater world?
3. At what age would you expect Jasmine to be able to put on her trousers or hat accurately?

J A S M I N E

A summary of Jasmine's development at 18 months

Physical development – gross

At 18 months:

- on holiday at the seaside, Jasmine walked and ran confidently on the sand
- she danced and moved rhythmically at the holiday centre music sessions
- she moved rhythmically to any sounds (e.g. the clock ticking, the washing machine whirring)
- her weight was now 8.6 kg (19 lb), placing her just below the second centile on her growth chart.

Physical development – fine

At 18 months:

- Jasmine clearly enjoyed sifting and trickling sand through her hands and fingers on the beach
- she filled and emptied her dumper truck over and over again.

Social and emotional development

At 18 months:

- Jasmine showed enjoyment on her first holiday at the seaside
- she cooperated well on the train and bus journeys to the holiday centre
- she woke very early on the first morning and was on the beach by 7 a.m.!
- Jasmine ate best when there was music playing, often requesting the radio at mealtimes
- when visiting other (familiar) people, Jasmine had a routine of pointing to her favourite items (e.g. at Granny's house this included a picture of the family dog, a china duck on a shelf, and a picture of a huge sunflower).

Intellectual, sensory and language development

At 18 months:

- Jasmine enjoyed watching out of the train window, and showed interest in what Mummy pointed out to her
- she loved the sand, and explored its properties well
- she clearly enjoyed the feel of sand, holding and trickling it between her fingers
- Jasmine repeatedly filled and emptied her dumper truck
- she insisted that seagulls were 'ducks'
- she was clearly fascinated by life-size models of Noddy and his 'friends' at the holiday centre, hugging them as she went past
- Jasmine vocalised urgently while bobbing up and down, to indicate that she wanted some music to be turned on
- she continued to enjoy books, and clearly had favourite pages (e.g. pictures of ducks, cats and flowers).

? Checkpoint questions

1. Why might Jasmine eat her meals better if listening to tapes or the radio?
2. Jasmine loves to look at the same books over and over again. How does this help the development of a toddler of this age?
3. What part do familiar items play in Jasmine's development?

Age: two years

Physical development – gross

At two years of age:

- toddlers run safely, starting and stopping with ease and generally avoiding obstacles
- they squat steadily while they play
- wheeled toys are pulled, showing an understanding of direction
- toddlers climb on and off furniture to look out of the window, through an open door, etc
- they walk upstairs (and often downstairs too) holding onto a handrail, both feet to each stair
- they propel a tricycle with their feet, but cannot as yet use pedals
- it is a very active and mobile stage in a toddler's development.

Physical development – fine

At two years of age:

- all fine movements are becoming increasingly skilful
- toddlers spoon-feed themselves well, with few spills
- they can often build six or seven bricks into a tower
- they can throw a small ball forward without falling over

- they 'walk' into a large ball when they try to kick it
- toddlers can often 'twist' their wrist to turn a door handle
- individual finger manipulation is emerging
- all five movements are becoming increasingly skilful.

Social and emotional development

At two years of age:

- toddlers spoon-feed themselves well, with few spills
- they lift and replace cups on surfaces
- they can put on clothing items such as a hat and shoes
- toddlers enjoy playing 'near' to others ('parallel play')
- they can be resistive and rebellious when frustrated or challenged, or when they are unable to make themselves understood ('the terrible twos')
- toddlers can be easily distracted from their tantrums
- toddlers defend their own possessions with determination
- they have no concept of sharing at this stage
- they can be resentful of attention shown towards others
- there is no understanding as yet of the need to defer their own wishes
- toddlers constantly demand attention
- they follow their carer around the home
- they cling tightly to their carer in tiredness, fear and frustration.

Intellectual, sensory and language development

At two years of age:

- toddlers are very curious about their environment
- enjoyment of story-books is evident
- toddlers can often build six or seven bricks into a tower
- they carry out simple instructions
- they role-play simple situations (e.g. making cups of tea, cooking dinner, etc.)
- simple jigsaws are coped with well
- toddlers usually draw vertical and horizontal lines, sometimes circles too
- a vocabulary of 50+ words is usual, often many more
- toddlers listen with a clear interest to others talking
- they put two or occasionally more words together in small phrases
- they refer to themselves by name
- toddlers talk to themselves in long monologues as they play
- many of their 'monologues' are not understood by others
- echolalia (repetition of words heard) is almost constant
- toddlers verbalise their needs – food, drink, toilet, toys, etc.
- toddlers like everything to be named for them
- they constantly name items (but names are not always recognisable)
- the use of one word or phrase may have more than one meaning.

A summary of Jasmine's development at 19 months

Physical development – gross

At 19 months:

- Jasmine really enjoyed ball games
- she could kick a football (not as yet with any force) while keeping her balance
- she loved chasing games
- she enjoyed pulling her caterpillar toy around
- she was very confident on her indoor slide.

Physical development – fine

At 19 months:

- Jasmine carefully picked daisies from the garden, and blew on them instead of sniffing them
- she tried to water flowers with her watering can, but managed to pour most of the water onto herself rather than on the flowers
- Jasmine loved water play – tipping, scooping and pouring water from container to container – making everything near to her very wet
- she could throw a large ball in her intended direction.

Social and emotional development

At 19 months:

- Jasmine initiated chasing games by squealing and running away, looking over her shoulder at whoever she wanted to chase her
- she enjoyed a special game with Granny under the flower arch, giggling as she pointed alternately to 'Jasmine' the person and 'jasmine' the flower.

Intellectual, sensory and language development

At 19 months:

- Jasmine had a new favourite word – 'flaa' (flower)
- she pointed out flowers everywhere she went
- Jasmine stopped to look at every flower (a walk in the garden took a long time at this stage in her development!)

- she understood that daisies could be picked but planted flowers must not be touched
- she used her dumper truck to collect items from around the garden (e.g. fallen apples, leaves, daisies, grass, etc.)
- Jasmine liked to place her beakers inside one another
- she also liked to build with her beakers
- Jasmine could build a tower of up to four bricks, but preferred to just add one each time, which she then removed before adding the next and therefore rarely built above two bricks high
- imitative play was emerging. Jasmine 'stirred' a cup of coffee with a plastic key and also gave her doll a ride on her tricycle.

A summary of Jasmine's development at 20 months

Physical development – gross

At 20 months:

- Jasmine continued to refine her large motor skills within her play
- she walked upstairs holding onto the handrail, both feet to each stair.

Physical development – fine

At 20 months:

- there were no significant changes in Jasmine's physical development
- she continued to refine her fine manipulative skills as she played.

Social and emotional development

At 20 months:

- Jasmine liked to hand out toys or other items to everyone present, and would then collect them in again
- she was very sociable with adults at toddler groups, also handing out and collecting items from them
- Jasmine loved to wear hats and to look at herself wearing them in the mirror
- she was shy when tired and liked a cuddle from the main adults in her life
- Jasmine moved house, and appeared to settle into her new environment well.

Intellectual, sensory and language development

At 20 months:

- Jasmine liked all items to be in their correct place (possibly linked to security and having moved house). She vocalised urgently if she considered things were 'wrong', insisting that:

- cereal packets must go back in the cupboard, not on the worktop
- cups should be placed on the table, not on the floor
- the kitchen mop must be upright
- the cows should be in the second field, not the field by the house!
- the stair gate at Granny's house should be shut as soon as she came through the front door

- Jasmine loved to play 'shopping' and took a bag with her wherever she went, filling it up with toys and objects (mostly toy fruit and vegetables), and emptying it out again
- Jasmine's latest words were 'bag', 'Mmmmm' ('Moo') in reference to the cows next door, 'Ffff' ('Woof') in response to any dog or picture of a dog, and 'sax' ('socks'), the term she uses for both shoes and socks.

? Checkpoint question

1. Why do you think children of Jasmine's age might be so insistent on everything being in its correct place?

A summary of Jasmine's development at 21 months

Physical development – gross

At 21 months:

- Jasmine continued to be active – running, climbing, dancing and playing energetically
- she could walk downstairs holding onto the handrail, both feet to each stair.

Physical development – fine

At 21 months:

- Jasmine showed a great interest in dressing and undressing. She could pull on her trousers, but at times put both feet in one leg
- she pulled tops over her head, occasionally managing to find both sleeves, but sometimes only one
- she was observed rummaging in the laundry basket where she proceeded to put on all six of the outfits she found, one on top of the other. Some of the tops were just round her neck, others she had managed to put on properly. She was very pleased with herself.

Social and emotional development

At 21 months:

- Jasmine liked to see adult approval for what she was doing (as with the six outfits from the laundry basket)
- signs of frustration were now visible from time to time, particularly when Jasmine was tired
- Jasmine had a tendency to throw things when annoyed or frustrated
- she began to crash her tricycle deliberately into things when 'cross'
- she became very shy with strangers (possibly as a result of moving house).

Intellectual, sensory and language development

At 21 months:

- Jasmine called 'miaow miaow miaow' (always three times) whenever she saw a cat
- she referred to sheep as 'baa', and her doll as 'beebee' ('baby')
- she called out 'wheresegone?' when the family cats ran away from her, always repeating it at least twice
- Jasmine played with 'beebee' a great deal, and liked to involve the doll in her play (e.g. she had to have reins on if in the pushchair and was very often given a cup of tea and sometimes the teapot too!)
- Jasmine copied Mummy's and Daddy's actions
- she enjoyed being allowed to play the piano.

? Checkpoint questions

1. Jasmine is beginning to imitate actions she sees, in her play. At what age is this most common?
2. What other examples of imitative play would you expect to see Jasmine demonstrate?
3. Jasmine had more teeth appear as she approached 21 months. Which teeth would you expect these to be?
4. When encouraging children of Jasmine's age to help dress themselves, what approach should adults take?
5. Frustration is a normal stage in toddler development. How should this be handled?
6. How is Jasmine's language likely to develop in the near future?

A summary of Jasmine's development at 22 months

Physical development – gross

At 22 months:

● greater physical control was seen as Jasmine helped to sweep up leaves in the garden, keeping good control of the broom

● she pulled a large sack up the garden for Grandad, and helped him to fill it with leaves and twigs.

Physical development – fine

At 22 months:

- Jasmine continued to be interested in dressing and undressing and some mornings was found with her pyjamas on backwards, or with only one sleeve in place, clearly exploring during the night
- she could now put on her socks, and put them on and took them off regularly throughout the day
- she started to use crayons regularly, making marks from side to side with occasional firm dots.

Social and emotional development

At 22 months:

- Jasmine shook her head saying 'Nonono' when she didn't want to do something, but could usually be coaxed quite easily
- she automatically put what she was playing with away when she was called, even if the floor was strewn with other toys
- she found a cup of orange juice one morning and gave Daddy a drink, even though he was still asleep!

Intellectual, sensory and language development

At 22 months:

- Jasmine regularly imitated those around her (e.g. she sat with her arms folded alongside Daddy, and occasionally unloaded the washing machine on her own initiative. One day she emptied the tumble dryer and put the washing into the washing machine, which showed good understanding of processes, despite being the wrong way round. She was seen holding up her jacket against the door frame imitating where an ironed shirt had been hung)
- she said 'Oh no', and 'Oh dear' when something went wrong, using both expression and emphasis
- Jasmine called out 'Doodles-dod-dod-voof-voof' in great excitement when she saw the dog (called Doodles) on the television programme, the 'Tweenies'
- she enjoyed watching children's television programmes while sitting alongside an adult.

A summary of Jasmine's development at 23 months

Physical development – gross

At 23 months:

- although Jasmine usually ran safely and well, she unfortunately ran into the corner of a wall and split her forehead open
- Jasmine could climb on and off furniture to reach the window blind, pulling the cord to lift it and see if Daddy's car had arrived.

Physical development – fine

At 23 months:

- Jasmine became fascinated by her nose, which her fingers explored regularly!
- when her breathing sounded 'odd' one day, Jasmine's mother looked carefully at her nose and found that two peas and a small piece of carrot had been poked up her nostrils! (Extremely careful supervision at mealtimes followed, and raisins were temporarily banned!)
- Jasmine could open some of the doors around the house, and locks and catches appeared on the kitchen cupboards and on the door to Daddy's office
- following her cut forehead, Jasmine picked off her butterfly stitches within about an hour! She is now likely to be left with a small scar.

Social and emotional development

At 23 months:

- Jasmine cried long and hard when she cut her forehead open, but cooperated with the medical professional who administered her stitches
- Jasmine sometimes liked to wear odd things to bed, such as a sun hat!

Intellectual, sensory and language development

At 23 months:

- Jasmine's language was evolving fast. Examples of some of the things she said included:
  - 'Mummy an a daddy in a car' (all said as one word)
  - 'tissue' and 'serrubbish' (when mopping up spills of her drinks)
  - 'dut der door?' ('Shall I shut the door?') and 'do der door' ('Please open the door')
  - 'dawdee' ('drawing'), 'fish' , 'bee', and 'beebee' ('baby', often while patting her tummy in an imitation of Mummy, who was pregnant at the time).

- Jasmine showed how at times toddlers have a very 'literal' understanding and interpretation of what is said to them. She usually clears away toys before getting into bed. One night the adult putting her to bed remarked that there were no toys to put away, so Jasmine promptly emptied out a toy box, and then helped to clear them up as usual!

❓ Checkpoint questions

1. Jasmine has begun to enjoy using crayons. What drawing actions might she be making?
2. Jasmine enjoys watching occasional television programmes alongside an adult. In what way is this adult involvement important to Jasmine's development?
3. As Jasmine approaches her second birthday, how many words would you expect her to be able to say?

A summary of Jasmine's development at two years

Physical development – gross

At two years of age:

- Jasmine's main Christmas present was a ball pool which she was immediately very active in, rolling around, diving into the balls, and trying to hide underneath them
- she had a doll's pram, which she pushed and pulled with (some) sense of direction
- she danced, hopped, jumped and rolled around the floor in active play
- Jasmine copied the actions that she had seen herself on a video made by Daddy
- Jasmine loved to bounce on her new bed
- she was extremely active for most of the time, and would rarely sit still.

Giving her elephant a ride

Physical development – fine

At two years of age:

- Jasmine could throw a small ball skilfully and easily, using an overarm gesture
- she was able to open most of her Christmas and birthday presents herself
- Jasmine cooked and made tea, putting cups on saucers, the lid on the teapot and so on
- she stirred the cups (Daddy takes sugar)
- Jasmine could turn door handles more easily now, and all the doors in the house needed fitting with safety catches!
- Jasmine loved to draw and chalk.

Social and emotional development

At two years of age:

- Jasmine thoroughly enjoyed both Christmas and her second birthday. She seemed unfazed by all the excitement and the change to her routine
- Jasmine clearly enjoyed playing with others in her ball pool
- she opened many of her presents while sitting in her ball pool, clearly indicating her enjoyment of her new 'special' place
- Jasmine slept in her new bed, which she loved, adjusting to it very well
- Jasmine hid behind the curtains, calling 'Where's Jaddy gone?'
- Jasmine occasionally indicated that she had 'done a poo', or was about to ('want a poo'), but was still not really interested in potty training
- Jasmine soon learned her parents' 'only two large toys' rule (see below).

Intellectual, sensory and language development

At two years of age:

- Jasmine soon learned to say 'ball pool', asking for it each morning
- Jasmine had some lovely toys, but for practical reasons her parents introduced a rule that she could only have two large toys (items like the slide, bike, pram, ball pool) out at a time. She accepted this very easily, and showed understanding within a few days by taking her tricycle to the store cupboard to 'exchange' it for something else
- Jasmine now said 'nanas yellow' ('bananas are yellow'), 'dawdy colours' and 'dawdy book' ('drawing colours' and 'drawing book' – a favourite birthday present)
- she also said 'ezza baby in a mummy' ('there's a baby in Mummy's tummy') while patting Mummy's bump
- Jasmine copied her actions accurately when watching a video of herself playing
- a lot of imitation play was noticeable. Jasmine cooked and carried out 'household' tasks such as vacuuming. She pressed the buttons on her toy kitchen microwave, saying 'beep beep', and turned the toy tap on saying 'pshhhh' for the water
- Jasmine loved to draw and now drew spirals, occasionally drawing where she shouldn't!
- Jasmine said 'Oh no, ne'er mind' when something went wrong (imitating the tolerant approach of her parents)
- she said 'Mummy's asheep' ('asleep'), 'the moo moos are asheep', 'Gandad's asheep', but she still called sheep 'baas'!
- having discovered the switch for the garden light Jasmine started to play 'moo moos light, moo moos dark' each evening until she could be lured away from the light switch
- Jasmine loved playing outside, particularly in the garden playhouse, busying herself with shopping, taking her toys for rides on her tricycle and in her pram, and drawing with her chalks.

A full range of Jasmine's language at the age of two years can be found on page 108–9.

Jasmine in her playhouse

❓ Checkpoint questions

1. Sometimes Jasmine likes to wear odd things to bed, such as a sun hat. Is this a problem do you think?
2. Accidents such as Jasmine's split forehead happen sometimes, despite the best of care and attention being received. What sensible precautions are needed with toddlers of Jasmine's age?
3. It was clear that Jasmine thoroughly enjoyed Christmas, but many toddlers can be quite irritable on such occasions. Why might this be the case?
4. Do you think that Jasmine is likely to have recognised herself in the video?
5. At what age should children be presented with rules or boundaries such as the one given to Jasmine regarding her large toys? Why are these important?
6. Jasmine still wears nappies in the day and at night. At what age does potty training usually take place?
7. Why might Jasmine call out 'Where's Jaddy gone?' when she is the one hiding?
8. How does imitative play help Jasmine in her development?
9. At what age are tantrums common?

JASMINE

An overview of Jasmine's development

Having read the development sections above, illustrating the development of toddlers in general and of Jasmine in particular, it can be seen that Jasmine is a very physical and dexterous little girl, who runs, climbs and plays well physically, and who uses fine manipulation skilfully. This was particularly seen in her interest in dressing and undressing herself.

After being considered 'small for dates' at birth, Jasmine has remained a child of slight build, who eats healthily but not hugely. She began to walk at an average age, she teethed later than many toddlers, and as this book goes to press she is still not all that interested in potty training. Jasmine appears to be too busy to be bothered!

Emotionally, Jasmine is a happy and secure little girl who enjoys a stable family life. She is sociable with children and adults alike at toddler groups and in similar situations, but becomes clingy when tired. Jasmine has a wonderful sense of humour, and loves to laugh and to make others laugh.

Regarding cognitive skills, Jasmine has a high level of understanding of all that goes on around her, and she shows this through her gestures, facial expressions and verbal queries. She has an extensive vocabulary, but much of it is in her own version of the English language. However, despite showing typical toddler inventiveness and some lack of clarity in her speech, Jasmine is mostly able to make herself understood. She is inquisitive and clearly likes to learn new names of objects when she encounters them for the first time. She likes also to repeat things to consolidate her understanding and uses a good range of sounds within her speech, without appearing to have any difficulties in pronunciation.

Jasmine has a good understanding of what is right, but sometimes chooses to test her boundaries. She has shown frustration occasionally when a problem arises, but is quite easily distracted from it again.

Shortly before this book went to press, Jasmine became a big sister to Harry Tobias. She was aged two years and four months. She appears to have accepted his arrival well. On her first visit to see Mummy and Harry in hospital Jasmine was initially more interested in the mother in the bed opposite, as she had a pink balloon tied to her baby's cot! Jasmine soon showed an interest in Harry, however, and held him for the first time when he was just 14 hours old.

Once Mummy and Harry were home from hospital, Jasmine spent a great deal of time watching her new brother. She repeatedly called 'Wake up Harry', adding 'Harry's awake' when he responded. She tested Harry's hearing well with her noises and he soon learned to sleep through most sounds. He headed his first ball when he was just three weeks old during some boisterous play in the ball pool!

Jasmine likes to help change Harry's nappy, passing wipes, nappies and clothing items. She kisses him and gives him cuddles, and is very impressed by the bright yellow content of his nappies, telling him 'Pretty poo, Harry!'

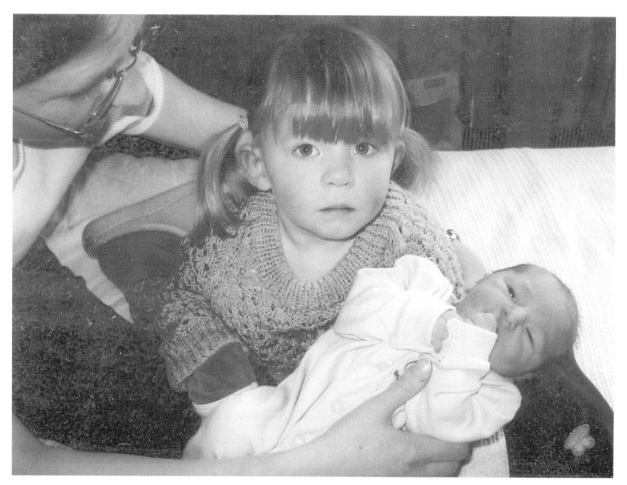

Jasmine first held Harry when he was fourteen hours old

Remember

★ You can continue to follow Jasmine's development at www.sandy-green.com

Also

★ *Nursery World* magazine will begin to feature the development of Jasmine's baby brother 'Harry Tobias' in a regular monthly column starting early in 2004

3 A brief look at developmental theories

Theories of development

There have been many theories about the way in which development takes place and what impacts upon children to influence their development or rate of development. Some of these theories have been touched upon in this chapter, with links to specific moments in Jasmine's development or an alternative example provided where applicable. However, this book is not intended to provide indepth discussion of psychology and related issues, so for readers who wish to explore the theories further, an easily accessible text on developmental psychology would be Cullis *et al.*'s *Psychology for You* (Nelson Thornes, 1999) or Cara Flanagan's *Applying Psychology to Early Child Development* (Hodder & Stoughton, 1996).

Assimilation and accommodation

Piaget's theory of assimilation and accommodation (discussed in Cullis *et al.* 1999) refers to the way in which a child initially has an understanding of one situation, which he is then able to apply to another, similar situation. For example, a child may understand that round green items in the fruit bowl are apples, but he will gradually move on to understand that round red items in the fruit bowl can also be apples.

JASMINE

Jasmine's development in relation to assimilation and accommodation theory

Jasmine's perception of dogs is relevant here. She first understood a dog to be large and black (the family Labrador, Charlie). She understood that large black dogs go 'woof woof'. She eventually applied this understanding to other large (black) dogs and then to large yellow dogs (golden retrievers). Eventually she was able to apply her understanding of what a dog *is* to smaller breeds too, and to dogs in a variety of colours.

Classical conditioning

The theory known as 'classical conditioning' was highlighted by Ivan Pavlov in 1902 (also discusssed in Cullis *et al.* 1999). He identified that dogs responded automatically (by producing saliva) when they were presented with food. This was a 'reflex behaviour', i.e. it was not learned. Pavlov experimented by starting to ring a bell when he was about to give the dogs food, and eventually just hearing the bell ring would cause the dogs to produce saliva.

Some people believe that babies can identify a link (through classical conditioning) between crying and being distressed. This would explain why it is often the case that if one baby is upset and in tears, other nearby infants will pick up on the distress and start to cry themselves.

Jasmine's development in relation to classical conditioning theory

Jasmine showed signs of classical conditioning when at 22 months she understood that pyjamas + bedtime = put away the toys. At this age she automatically put whatever she was playing with into the toy box as soon as she was called. Another example is: ever since she has been able to sit securely she has been encouraged to move to music, and she now dances instantly to any rhythmic sound she hears wherever she may be.

Operant conditioning

B. F. Skinner highlighted the theory of operant conditioning through an experiment using rats in a box. A hungry rat would sniff and scuttle around until eventually, purely by chance, it touched a lever (positioned by Skinner) which released a pellet of food. The rat soon learned that in order to get its 'reward' it needed to press the lever, and having realised this, it pressed the lever more frequently. (For further discussion see Cullis *et al.* 1999.)

Children will respond similarly to any positive reinforcement they receive, such as a pleasurable response in return for an action.

Jasmine's development in relation to operant conditioning theory

Jasmine is praised regularly, which reinforces effort, achievement and good behaviour. Signs of operant conditioning can be seen when she clears up any water she happens to spill when trying to drink out of a cup without a lid. She has been praised for 'mopping up' the water (which she loves doing) and now automatically asks for a tissue (sheet of kitchen roll) whenever she makes a mess.

Gender stereotyping

In the earliest years, children gain an awareness of being male or female. This is known as their 'sex identity'. As they gradually learn what is expected of them by the adults who care for them, they develop their 'gender identity'. Powerful influences on gender identity can include adults who encourage boys to be more active, independent and emotionally reserved than girls, or adults who urge girls to be more caring and don't encourage the same level of independence as they would in boys. Situations like these have a negative impact on children's understanding of their own and others' gender identities and on their concept of 'what is male' and 'what is female'.

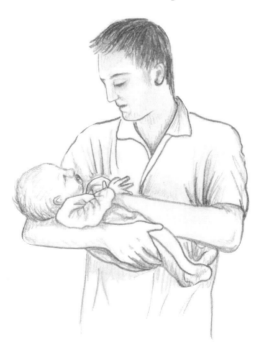

A positive role model

There have been experiments carried out in which adults have been given a baby to hold and play with. Each baby has been dressed in either blue or pink. A marked difference emerged in the ways in which the adults handled and stimulated the babies, generally displaying a calmer and more soothing approach towards the babies in pink. This research showed how an infant's behaviour (and gender identity) later on in childhood might well be affected by how an adult treats the child in the earliest months.

Jasmine's development in relation to gender stereotyping

As she approached the age of two years, Jasmine began to show an occasional awareness of the differences between men/boys and women/girls, by correctly pointing to pictures of them in her books when asked, although she still sometimes thought that women with short hair were men! In doing so she was showing the first signs of sex stereotyping.

It is unlikely that at this age she would have had any great understanding of roles, stereotypical or otherwise, but these would gradually develop over time. For example, as Jasmine's mother is at home full time and does not drive, and her father goes out to work and always drives the car, Jasmine could well develop some fixed gender role stereotypes within her own family. Her parents do share the cooking and some of the household tasks, however, and are both involved in caring for Jasmine, so one would hope that this would give her a broader understanding of gender norms.

It will be important to Jasmine's learning that she reads books and sees pictures showing women driving cars and working, and men at home carrying out household tasks and playing with children, to ensure that she acquires as full a non-stereotyped image of gender role as possible.

To date, Jasmine has a range of toys and activities that could be classed as completely non-gender specific. She has a doll, cooking pans and a tea set (stereotypically girls' toys) and clearly loves brushing hair, cooking and making tea, but she equally enjoys her cars, construction materials and football (stereotypically boys' toys) and plays, builds and runs around with enormous amounts of energy. For examples of Jasmine's toys and an overview of the stages of play linked to development see the 'Stimulating play' section in Chapter 4.

Object permanence

In the context of child development, the term 'object permanence' is used in relation to an infant who has developed a degree of cognitive maturity. If a three-month-old has been looking at a toy which is then covered over by an adult, the infant will lose interest and look away because he has not yet learned that the object is still actually there despite being hidden. The child has not yet achieved 'object permanence'. However, an older infant (from about eight to nine months onwards) would have reached out to try to uncover the toy. This awareness that the toy is still there even though it cannot be seen means that the child has acquired object permanence.

Jasmine's development in relation to object permanence

At around eight months old Jasmine was able to find toys and other items that she had seen covered up by other family members. She clearly found this to be a good game. Playing 'Peekabo' with Jasmine also contributed to the development of object permanence, as bit by bit she began to understand that while covering up the face, the person behind the hands still remained constant.

Attachment, separation and bonding

To bond with someone is to form a relationship with them, and most babies form a bond with whoever cares for them most. This is 'attachment'. Humans seem to be pre-programmed to form these attachments, with babies easily gaining the attention of those around them and bringing out the 'need to nuture' instinct in most adults, with their appealing looks and lusty cries.

In the earliest weeks of life babies respond to most adults with whom they have contact, but are more easily settled by their main carers. From two months onwards, they enjoy the company of any adults, but smile more readily for their main carers.

By the time they reach eight months, infants often begin to show anxiety if separated from their main carers ('separation anxiety'). As time goes on, however, most infants form attachments with a number of carers.

Jasmine's development in relation to attachment, separation and bonding

Jasmine did not show separation anxiety at the usual age. This is most likely to have been due to her family's living arrangements at the time. From the time that she was born there had been several adults in the house, all of whom she was very familiar with, and this meant that whenever her parents left her she was still being cared for by adults she lived with. At about a year old, and having moved from the maternal family home, Jasmine protested briefly on one or two occasions when left by her parents, but soon settled down to play. Their return was always greeted with delight.

Social learning theory

Social learning theory relates to how children's behaviour and actions are affected by what they see and/or experience. For example, if a child thinks that someone is rewarded positively for doing something (by being given attention, praised, etc.), he may try to copy the action himself. Alternatively, if a child sees a negative response being made (punishment, disinterest, being ignored by the adult, etc.) he is less likely to copy the action.

Similarly, if a child's own (unwanted) behaviour is consistently ignored, it is likely to diminish. If, however, it always gets the adult's attention, it is likely to continue. A balance needs to be struck between what can safely (and practically) be ignored and what needs to be responded to. When shaping and managing a child's behaviour it is important to provide clear and consistent boundaries, keeping these to a minimum. A few firmly established boundaries provide greater understanding and security for a child than a lot of boundaries that are sometimes upheld and sometimes not.

Jasmine's development in relation to social learning theory

At a very young age (four months) Jasmine would respond with laughs and smiles whenever she saw her bunny (her favourite cuddly toy at the time). Her body language showed anticipation whenever the toy was produced, and by tickling her with the bunny each time she reached for it, the game of action and re-action was established. Her bunny became known as 'Posi-bunny' (short for 'positive reinforcement').

As an inquisitive toddler always exploring her environment, Jasmine soon learned which cupboards in the kitchen she was allowed to take things out of (those containing plastic bowls, cups, etc.), and which she must only look at (those containing china, glasses, cooking pans, etc.) through the comments and guidance of her family, again as a result of positive reinforcement.

Language development

Language development impacts on every other area of a person's development, and children need to understand the importance of interacting with others before they communicate in whatever form they choose.

There have been conflicting theories on how language develops, with some theorists claiming that language development is dependent on an infant's cognitive (intellectual) development, and others feeling that language needs to be established for learning to take place. The question 'Is language dependent on thought, or is thought dependent on language?' has been asked many times.

The main theories regarding language development can be briefly summarised as follows:

- *Association theory*: the child gradually builds up his repertoire of language by associating words with what he sees, for example learning that a teddy is a teddy, or a dog is a dog. This theory does not, however, explain how a child learns to describe his own feelings or emotions.
- *Biological theory*: the child absorbs the language he hears, decodes it, and develops an understanding of its rules through what is referred to as the 'language acquisition device' (LAD).
- *Behaviourist theory*: the child's language is shaped by adults' responses to the noises he makes. For example, the infant who says 'Mamama' repeatedly will be likely to repeat this again and again if an adult responds by saying 'Yes, Mummy will be coming soon'. The sounds are being reinforced for the child.
- *Maturational theory*: the child's language will simply develop as he goes along, providing he hears language in various forms (e.g. speech, radio, etc.).
- *Interactionist theory*: a child's language reflects what he has experienced as well as what he understands.

Jasmine's development in relation to language development theory

It has always been clear that Jasmine could understand an enormous amount about her environment long before she was able to articulate anything using language in a recognisable form. She moved through the main stages of non-verbal communication, speech-like noises and imitation, responding to the encouragement of the adults in her life. From about 21 months old, more and more new words appeared, evidencing the breadth and depth of her knowledge and understanding. Jasmine's language links predominantly with the interactionist theory of language development (experience and understanding) together with behaviourist theory (reinforcement by adults' responses).

By two years of age Jasmine was using short (often disjointed) phrases. Some of her phrases made complete sense, whereas others still needed some deciphering. For a chart of Jasmine's language use and development see Tables 3.2 and 3.3 on pages 108–9.

Stages of language development

The process of language development can be divided into ten separate stages. Although children will develop language at their own rate, they will each pass through the language stages in the same order. These stages are as follows:

1. Non-verbal communication/expression
2. Speech-like noises
3. Controlling sounds, using mouth and tongue
4. Imitating sounds
5. First words
6. Development of vocabulary (50 words at two years of age, often more)
7. Putting words together to form simple phrases and sentences
8. Use of grammar
9. Use of meaning
10. Using language to develop other skills, for example early literacy.

Table 3.1 links the ten stages to approximate ages, but it must be remembered that these vary considerably from child to child. An overview of Jasmine's language development is provided in Table 3.2 for purposes of comparison.

Table 3.1 Language development

Age	Understanding	No. of words	Type of words or sounds	Average length of sentence
3 mths	Soothed by sound	0	Cooing and gurgling	0
6 mths	Responds to voice tones	0	Babbling	0
1 year	Knows own name and a few others	1	Noun (Naming word)	1 word
18 mths	Understands simple commands	6–20	Nouns	1 word
2 years	Understands much more than he can say	50+	Verbs and pronouns (Action + name)	1–2 word phrases
2½ years	Enjoys simple and familiar stories	200+	Pronouns: I, me, you Questions: What, Where	2–3 word phrases
3 years	Carries out complex commands	500–1,000	Plurals Verbs in present tense Questions: Who	3–4 word phrases
4 years	Listens to long stories	1,000–1,500	Verbs in past tense Questions: Why, Where, How	4–5 word sentences
5 years	Developing the ability to reason	1,500–2,000	Complex sentences with adult forms of grammar	

Table 3.2 Jasmine's language development

Age	Understanding	No. of words	Type of words or sounds	Average length of sentence
3 mnths	Calmed by Mummy's voice and by music (Pachelbel's Canon and Sinead O'Connor)	0	Chuckles, coos and gurgles conversationally, turn-taking with adults.	0
6 mnths	Responds to familiar voices	0	Babbles almost incessantly, mainly using the sounds 'ummm' and 'yi yi yi'	0
1 year	Knows own name and a few others	2	'In air?' ('Who's in there?' or 'What's that?') 'dor' ('dog') 'hooray'	1 word
18 mnths	Repeats her own new word – 'gollygollygollygolly' Understands 'car' and 'duck'	8	Nouns plus gobbledegook	1 word
2 years	Understands much of what is said to her Enjoys simple and familiar stories	Approx. 120 Some clear, some less so	Verbs and pronouns, e.g. 'Mummy fine it' ('Mummy find it'), 'Daddy a gate' ('Daddy's opening/shutting the gate'), 'boon in sky' ('the hot air balloon is in the sky')	2–3 word phrases, e.g. 'bean a sausee' ('beans and sausages'), 'cackas a chee' ('crackers and cheese'), 'socks a pink' ('the socks are pink')

At two years of age Jasmine's language included the words listed (with translations) in Table 3.3. There are now a lot more objects that Jasmine is able to name in her picture books, when out shopping, and so on.

Table 3.3 Jasmine's vocabulary at two years old

Word/phrase	Translation	Word/phrase	Translation
norange/nor'n	orange	Teedies yo'ya	Tweenies yoghurt
boo	blue	la la	apple
pink		gapes	grapes
perpa	purple	ray i' bowl	raisins in a bowl
gee	green	cackas a chee	crackers and cheese
colour?	what colour is it?	bean a toe	beans on toast
socks a pink	the socks are pink	bean a sausee	beans and sausages
sock colour?	what colour are the socks?	high	highchair
nanas yellow	bananas are yellow	where strap gone?	(when her highchair straps are in the wash)
moo moos	cows		
dod	dog	Mummy geddit	Mummy get it
n'/dree	drink	Mummy fine it	Mummy find it
wo-wo	water	Mummy el	Mummy help
n' a fee	drink in the fridge	dawdy colours	crayons
yo'ya	yoghurt	dawdy book	colouring book

Word/phrase	Translation	Word/phrase	Translation
dawdy talks	chalks	ergh, dirty	this is dirty
Oh no, ne'er mind		baas	bath
ezza baby in a mummy		bot	bottom (includes girls' and boys' 'bits' and bottoms)
I dropped it	I've dropped, spilled or thrown something	poo on pot	poo on the potty
dropped it	(including falling over and hair blowing around)	wee	
		c'eam	nappy cream/cream on grazed knees, etc.
Daddy in car		mat	changing mat
Daddy in shower		mats a fee'	fridge magnets
Daddy a work	Daddy is at work	Mummy in air	Mummy, I want you to come in here/go in there
Daddy fuwwy	Daddy is funny		
Daddy 'ome	Daddy is home	a stairs	I want to go up/down stairs
Daddy a gate	Daddy is opening/shutting the gate	up – down	(putting her arms by her sides or on her tummy)
Mummy's asheep	Mummy's asleep		
Gandad's a heep	Grandad's asleep	down – up	(arms in the air)
moo moos are asheep	cows are asleep (lying down, or at night)	fivvish	I have finished
		oh this	oh, there it is
moo moos light, moo moos dark	(when turning the garden light switch on and off)	door shut	the door is shut/I'm shutting the door/I want you to shut the door
where Gandad gone	where's Grandad gone?	boon in sky	the hot air balloon is in the sky/helium balloon touching the ceiling
Ganny	Granny		
Beebee	Baby (her doll)		
o'	hot		

Use of consonants

The usual sequential development of consonants in English is as follows:

at 2 years → m n p b t d w
at 2 ½ years → k g ng (as in 'sing') h
2 ½–3 years → f s l y

Although there are many of her own variations of words within her vocabulary, at two years old Jasmine uses a good range of consonants. She uses each of the above sounds, except for 'ng' and 'l'.

? **Checkpoint questions**

1. What are the main stages of language development?
2. On average, how many words can a two-year-old speak?
3. What is 'object permanence'?
4. What is 'echolalia'?

4 Caring for babies and toddlers

Caring for babies and toddlers takes time, commitment and stamina. They need a combination of physical and emotional care. This involves giving them attention, love and time, and showing them that you find pleasure in being with them. A baby that feels wanted and secure within his relationship with his main carer(s) is likely to be a happy baby or toddler. Table 4.1 identifies the different aspects of caring for a baby or toddler that will be covered in this chapter. For more information on these topics see Green (2000).

Table 4.1 Important aspects of care

Types of care	Examples
Intimate care	Nappy changing, washing, bathing
Nutritional care	Feeding, weaning
Physical care	Skin, hair, teeth, feet, suitability of clothing, maintaining correct body temperature, lighting, ventilation
Preventative care	Preventing cross-infection, good personal hygiene, safety, immunisation programmes
Communication	Talking, singing, smiles, gestures, touch, massage
Providing stimulation	Through various objects including mobiles, mirrors, music boxes, treasure baskets, books and toys

Intimate care

When dealing with body fluids of any kind, hygiene must always be of utmost importance. This particularly applies to nappy changing. Staff in day care settings use disposable gloves, but at home good personal hygiene practice should be sufficient.

Most babies are 'topped and tailed' in the mornings and bathed in the evening before being put to bed. Topping and tailing involves washing the face and refreshing the top half of the body, before finishing off with a nappy change.

Topping and tailing

Preparation

It is important to get everything ready in advance. You will need:

- a towel
- a changing mat
- a bowl of cooled boiled water

- a bowl of warm water
- some cotton wool
- a barrier cream (if used)
- a clean nappy
- a fresh set of clothes
- access to a nappy bucket (for towelling nappies), or
- a nappy sack (if using disposables)
- access to the laundry basket for clothes.

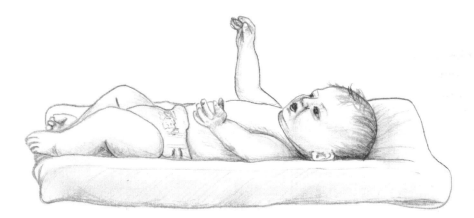

Method

1. Place the baby on a changing mat and undress to his vest and nappy.
2. Using the cooled boiled water, wipe each eye from the nose corner outwards, using each piece of cotton wool no more than once.
3. Repeat two or three times for each eye.
4. Dry the eye area delicately with corner of a clean towel.
5. Carefully clean the ears and around the face using moistened cotton wool, ensuring that you reach all the creases, particularly under the chin and behind the ears. Dry gently.
6. Using a larger piece of moistened cotton wool, freshen up the baby's armpits and hands, removing all fibres collected between the fingers. Dry gently.
7. In newborn babies check that the umbilical stump is clean, but do not wash or handle it unnecessarily. Whenever possible, it should be left alone (they tend to shrivel up and drop off 7 to 10 days after birth).
8. Remove the soiled nappy and place in a bucket or nappy sack.
9. Clean the nappy area thoroughly with warm water (or baby wipes if used), ensuring that you clean all creases, wiping from the front to the back.
10. Put on a clean nappy (applying barrier cream if used), dress the baby and have a cuddle!

> **Points to remember**
>
> ★ Always wipe from the front to the back when cleansing a girl's nappy area as this avoids any infection being passed from the bowels to the vaginal area.
> ★ Cleansing of a boy's nappy area does not necessitate the pulling back of the foreskin. Excessive cleaning can actually cause irritation and infection, rather than preventing it.

Changing a baby's nappy

Once a decision has been made regarding what type of nappies are to be used, the appropriate equipment needs to be gathered together.

Disposable nappies are easy to use and can be very absorbent, but they are expensive and many people are concerned about the impact of their use on the environment. Towelling nappies are cheaper to use, but they have to be washed and dried, which is not always so convenient. In many areas of the country there are now nappy laundering services. These often appeal to environmentally conscious parents, who do not have the time (or inclination) to do the nappy washing themselves. Towelling nappies can be bought ready 'shaped', or in squares that need to be folded. Figure 4.1 (pages 113–15) shows three examples of different ways to fold a towelling nappy.

Bathing a baby

Bathing a baby can be carried out using two different methods: the 'traditional' method and the 'modern' method.

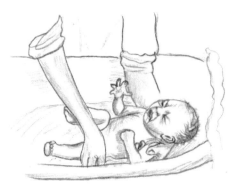

Everything must be prepared in advance. The temperature of the room should be at least 20 °C (68 °F), with windows and doors closed to prevent drafts. The bath should be placed securely in a special bath stand or on a firm surface such as the floor. Many people choose to place it inside the family bath.

Towelling nappies (1)

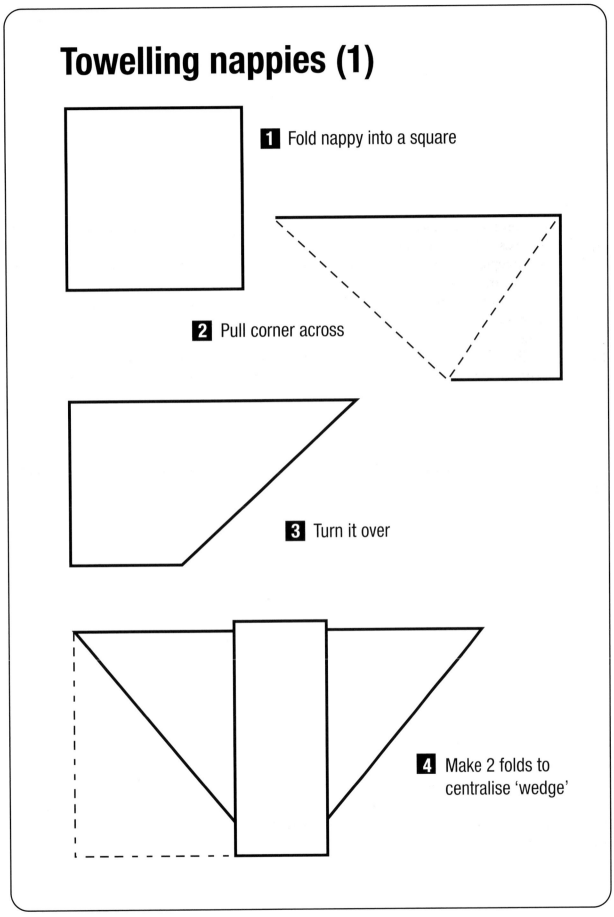

1 Fold nappy into a square

2 Pull corner across

3 Turn it over

4 Make 2 folds to centralise 'wedge'

Figure 4.1 Examples of how to fold a towelling nappy

Towelling nappies (2)

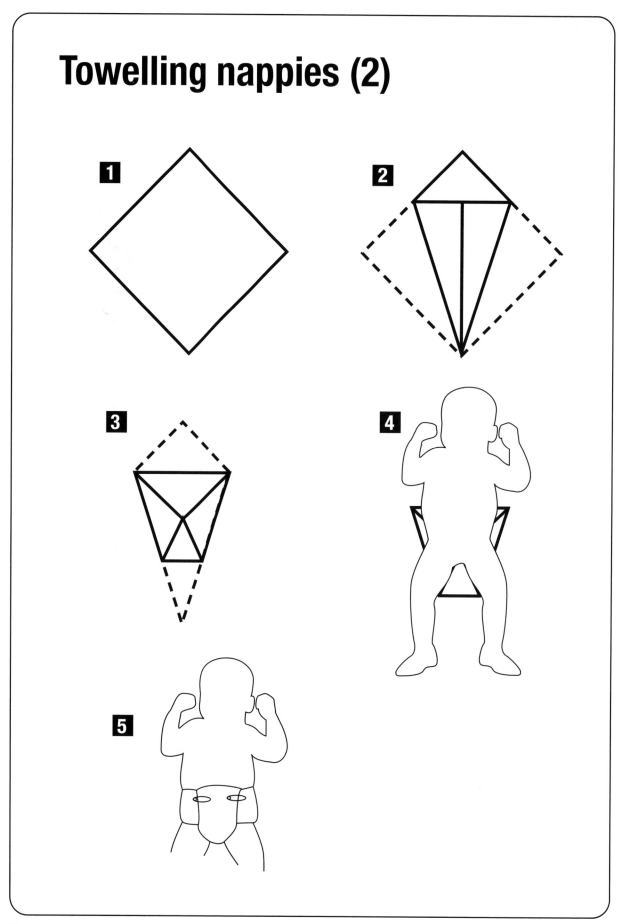

Figure 4.1   Examples of how to fold a towelling nappy (continued)

Towelling nappies (3)

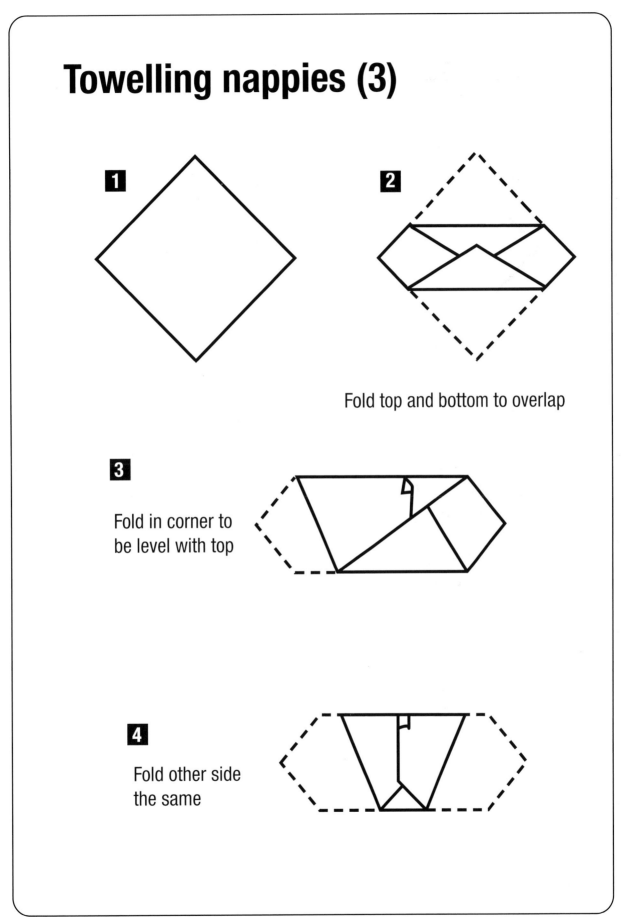

1

2

Fold top and bottom to overlap

3

Fold in corner to
be level with top

4

Fold other side
the same

Figure 4.1   Examples of how to fold a towelling nappy (continued)

Preparation

You will need:

- a baby bath, with water at 37 °C (98.6 °F). ALWAYS use a bath thermometer to check the water temperature before putting the baby in
- changing mat
- towels
- cotton wool
- a bowl of cooled boiled water for washing the baby's eyes
- shampoo (if used)
- soap
- barrier cream (if used)
- a clean nappy
- a fresh set of clothes
- access to a nappy bucket (for towelling nappies), or
- a nappy sack (if using disposables)
- access to a laundry basket for clothing.

Traditional method

1. Undress the baby to just his nappy and wrap him in the towel with the top corner folded away from you.
2. Wash his eyes and face following the topping and tailing guidelines in the previous section.
3. Hold the baby over the bath (still wrapped in the towel) under your arm, resting him on your hip.
4. Gently wet the baby's hair all over.
5. Add shampoo or soap and rub in gently but firmly.
6. Rinse the hair by leaning the baby backwards over the bath, drying the hair with the folded-over corner of the towel.
7. Lay the baby across your lap and remove his nappy, cleansing away excess faeces. ALWAYS keep hold of the baby by firmly grasping the arm and shoulder furthest away from you. Even very young babies can move suddenly.

8. With your spare hand, gently wet and soap the baby all over, turning him by pulling him over towards you, holding shoulder and thigh, and onto his tummy. When you have finished soaping the back and bottom, turn the baby again in the same way (always towards you).

9. Supporting the baby's head and neck with one hand and his bottom with the other, lower him into the bath.

10. Gently rinse the baby all over, continually supporting the head and neck with your wrist, and holding his shoulder and arm.

11. When ready for drying, lift the baby onto your lap, wrap in the towel and cuddle dry!

12. Apply nappy and clothing as before.

13. Brush or groom hair as appropriate.

14. Trim nails as necessary using blunt baby scissors (carers will need parents' permission to do this).

Points to remember

★ Babies usually have a feed after a bath and are then put down to sleep.
★ Carers should only use talcum powder if parents insist. It has been suggested that it may be linked to the development of asthma in early childhood.
★ Cultural practice regarding hair care, use of oils and creams should be adhered to by carers.
★ NEVER poke cotton buds into ears, noses and so on.
★ Babies need continuous supervision by a responsible adult at all times when being bathed.

Modern method

1. Bath water, clothing and so on should be prepared in the same way as for the traditional method.

2. Start by adding a bathing preparation (a suitable baby bathing lotion) to the water.

3. Lower the baby into the water after the eyes and face have been washed.

4. Soap the baby using the 'bubble bath' water in which he is sitting.

5. Continue the process as for the traditional method above.

Points to remember

★ Using a bathing preparation can make the water (and baby) quite slippery, so particular care is needed in holding the baby.
★ If a bathing preparation causes irritation of the baby's skin do not continue to use it.
★ Some preparations irritate babies' skin in the early weeks after birth, but can be used without problems later on.

Bathing older babies

From seven or eight months onwards, babies usually progress into the family bath, although some babies prefer the security of the baby bath for far longer than this. Babies of this age are usually much more active than younger infants and will appreciate having more room to splash and play at bathtime. By this time most babies are able to sit alone quite well, but it should be remembered that water makes them buoyant, and you will need to be ready to support them if they slip.

Points to remember

★ The precautions taken when bathing younger infants, regarding temperature, preparation and supervision, also apply when bathing older children.
★ It is important to ensure that the baby cannot reach the hot tap, as this remains hot for some time after use.
★ Do not fill the bath too full. If the water is too deep, the baby will float.
★ Sitting on a rubber mat can help a baby feel more secure.
★ A range of containers and bath toys will keep the baby amused and stimulated.
★ Many babies enjoy bathing with a parent.

Fear at bathtime

At times a baby may become fearful of water. This may be due to a previous incident such as:

● slipping in the bath
● water getting in the eyes
● stinging eyes from soaps or shampoos.

To counteract any anxiety always ensure that you:

● never leave babies alone in a bath
● always hold babies securely when they are in the bath
● never allow babies to try to stand
● always use non-stinging products especially designed for babies' delicate skin
● use a hair ring to keep water out of their eyes, if they dislike the sensation
● do not make a big issue of bathing if it becomes a battle. Often if you omit the bath or the hair wash for a couple of days, the issue will disappear, as the baby 'forgets' it was a problem.

Point to remember

★ Although most parents and carers like to freshen their babies up with a bath at the end of each day, it is not absolutely essential. A good wash using the top and tail method can also maintain good levels of cleanliness.

Nutritional care

The nutritional care of babies and toddlers involves the earliest choice between either breast- or bottle-feeding, and also the introduction of solid foods, which is a process known as 'weaning'. For the first four to six months most babies will need only milk feeds, either breast or bottle, as this usually gives them all the nutrients required to support their growth and development. On occasions, babies are weaned onto solid foods before the age of four months, but this should only be undertaken on the advice of a health visitor or paediatrician.

Let's start by examining the advantages and disadvantages of both types of milk feed (see Table 4.2).

Table 4.2 Breast-feeding or formula-feeding?

Advantages of breast-feeding	Advantages of bottle-feeding
The balance of breast milk nutrients is perfect for the infant	Feeding routines can be shared
The milk 'matures' with the baby, constantly meeting his needs	Siblings can be more directly involved
Breast milk offers a degree of immunity against infection in the earliest weeks	Can be less tiring for the mother
	It is easy to see how much milk the baby has had
Breast milk protects against eczema, asthma and jaundice	The mother can leave her baby for a while, knowing that his feeding needs will be met
Breast-feeding helps the mother to regain her figure more quickly	
Breast-fed babies have less gastroenteritis and fewer chest infections	Formula can now be bought ready made up
The baby's nappies are less smelly	
There is a lower risk of diabetes later on	
Breast milk is always 'on hand'	
Breast milk is cheaper – the milk is free!	

Disadvantages of breast-feeding	Disadvantages of bottle-feeding
Only the mother can feed, lessening the opportunities to involve siblings and others	Formula milk lacks the immunological qualities of breast milk
The mother can become over-tired as she has to cover all the night feeds herself	There is always a risk of bacterial infection from teats, bottles, etc.
There is no record of how much milk the infant has had. This is judged by contentment	Making up feeds correctly is vital to ensure a correct balance is achieved
There is always a possibility of feeding problems such as mastitis, sore nipples, etc.	Over-diluting a feed leads to a hungry baby
	Over-concentrated feeds can harm a baby
The mother needs a good healthy diet	Formula feeds need to be bought
The mother needs support/feeding bras	A range of equipment is needed for both feeding and sterilising
Breast pads may need to be bought	

Breast-feeding

Breast milk is considered by all health care staff as the best option for every baby. It offers the infant some natural protection from disease or infection through the mother's own immunity, and it is considered to be nature's 'designer food', since breast milk changes to accommodate each child's developing needs as the infant grows. The early milk is rich in colostrum and offers the infant some protection against common infections. A mother is encouraged to breast-feed for the first few days in order to give her child these benefits even when she is not intending to breast-feed on a long-term basis.

Breast-fed babies vary considerably in the length of time they suck at the breast. Some are able to take all they need in just a few minutes whereas others will want to suck for far longer. Allowing the infant to 'set the pace' of feeding helps to prevent engorgement of the breasts. At each feed the baby will initially receive the 'fore' milk, which offers satisfaction in the short term, but the richer 'hind' milk that follows often gives satisfaction for a longer period. The usual practice is for babies to feed from alternate breasts at consecutive feeds.

Points to remember

★ Feeding babies on demand ensures that they are able to satisfy their hunger.
★ Babies who sleep well in between feeds are usually getting sufficient nutrients.
★ When breast-feeding, it is difficult to know how much milk a baby has had, so regular weighing helps to monitor this and gives the mother peace of mind.
★ If an infant has green slimy stools it may indicate that he is not getting enough milk and longer or more frequent feeds may need to be encouraged.
★ Breast-feeding mothers need to support their backs well.
★ When breast-feeding, ensure the baby sucks with his lips curled back, taking the whole of the areola into the mouth (although different-shaped breasts will necessitate different angles for feeding).
★ Bonding is enhanced during feeding by the eye contact made between mother and child. As the infant develops he also starts to pat his mother's breast contentedly.

Formula-feeding

The alternative to breast-feeding is to use formula feeds. These can be bought ready prepared, but most parents choose to make them up themselves.

Formula milk is an extremely good alternative to breast milk. As an infant's nutritional needs change, the parents need to make relevant alterations to the formula they use. This is linked to the growth rate of their baby and his levels of hunger. In early years settings, babies' feeds will usually be supplied ready prepared by the parents and stored in a refrigerator until needed.

> **Point to remember**
>
> ★ Individual babies must have their feeds labelled clearly and these should be stored separately to avoid confusion or cross-infection.

Making a formula feed

Preparation

You will need:

- formula feed
- bottle
- teats
- knife
- kettle (pre-boiled).

> **Points to remember**
>
> ★ Wash your hands thoroughly before handling any feeding equipment.
> ★ Prepare feeds on a clean surface.
> ★ Have spare teats handy in case you drop one.

Method

1. Boil the kettle in advance.
2. Remove bottle from steriliser unit and rinse with boiled water.
3. Pour sufficient cooled boiled water into the bottle for the feed required (1 fl oz of boiled water for each scoop of formula).
4. Check the liquid level is accurate.
5. Open the tin of formula.
6. Using the scoop enclosed in the tin, add the correct number of scoops to the bottle, levelling each one off with a flat knife.
7. If the bottle is to be used straight away, put on the teat, ring and lid, and shake gently to dissolve the formula.
8. After checking the temperature on the inside of your wrist, the feed is ready for use.
9. If storing the feed for later on, put a disc and ring on the bottle and shake gently to mix.
10. Remove disc and replace with upside-down teat (DO NOT allow formula to touch the teat, as bacteria may begin to form).
11. Cover with disc and lid, and refrigerate the bottle until needed.

Points to remember

★ It is important that the scoops of formula are level.
★ Heaped or 'packed down' scoops lead to over-feeding, which can in turn lead to excessive weight gain, high levels of salt intake and possible kidney strain.
★ Too few scoops of formula or too much water can lead to over-dilution and under-feeding. Under-feeding can lead to poor weight gain and a hungry baby.
★ A baby needs 75 ml of formula per 500 g of body weight (2½ fl oz per pound) in each 24-hour period.
★ It is easier to make up enough feeds for the day all in one go, providing suitable refrigeration is available. This is particularly useful for families with twins or other multiples.

Giving a formula feed

Before feeding the baby it is important to ensure that everything you might need is to hand. You should be seated comfortably and able to give the baby your full attention. Often an infant will be more comfortable having had a nappy change prior to feeding, but individual routines will vary.

Method

1. Make sure your hands are clean before touching the feeding equipment and beginning the feed.
2. Have all equipment together and suitably covered.
3. The bottle can be kept warm in a jug of hot water while you settle your baby.
4. Hold the baby close to you, offering a sense of security and pleasure to the infant.
5. Test the temperature of the formula against the inside of your wrist. It should feel warm, not hot.
6. Check that the milk is flowing at the appropriate rate for the baby you are feeding. Several drops per second is usual, but rates do vary from baby to baby.
7. Encourage the onset of feeding by touching the teat against the baby's lips before placing the teat into the mouth.
8. Milk should always cover the whole teat to stop the baby taking in excess air and becoming frustrated at not receiving enough milk with each suck.
9. If the baby is reluctant to suck, pull the teat away gently. The tension of this will often give the baby the impetus to suck harder.
10. About half way through the feed, stop and wind the baby (see below).
11. Wind again when the feed is over and settle the baby down to sleep. At this point another nappy change may be required.
12. When a baby has finished feeding, any remaining formula should be discarded and the bottle washed thoroughly before it is placed in a steriliser.

Point to remember

★ Always throw away left over milk and NEVER use the same bottle twice without sterilising it.

Winding

To help babies release any trapped air swallowed during feeding, they need to be winded. To do this they are best held in an upright position to allow the air to 'rise'. Useful positions for this include the following:

- Sitting the baby forward so he is resting against your hand, while you rub or gently pat his back with your other hand.
- Placing the baby on your shoulder and rubbing or gently patting him.
- Resting the baby in a prone position (on his tummy) and rubbing his back. Very young babies can be rested along your arm, while older babies can be laid prone across your lap.

Points to remember

★ It is always useful to have a cloth handy as many babies posset (regurgitate) some milk during the winding process.
★ The head and neck of young babies should always be well supported.

Sterilising

Bottles and all other feeding utensils need sterilising to prevent illness occurring due to the growth and ingestion of bacteria. There are various methods to choose from:

- cold water sterilisers
- steam sterilisers
- microwave sterilisers
- boiling method.

Cold water sterilisers

There are two alternatives available if this method is chosen: sterilising solution or sterilising tablets. With either option the steriliser needs to be filled to the required capacity with cold water and the sterilising solution or tablet added (and allowed to dissolve) before adding bottles and other feeding equipment. Each bottle, teat or other item needs to be fully submerged, and held under water by a 'float'. Items can be considered to be sterile 30 minutes from the time the last piece of equipment has been added. The solution needs to be replaced every 24 hours. Most sterilising tanks are large enough to hold a considerable amount of feeding equipment (Figure 4.2).

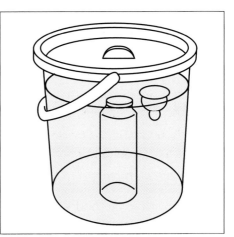

Figure 4.2 A cold water steriliser unit

Point to remember

★ All items must be fully submerged. When sterilising bottles it is important to ensure that all the air bubbles have been released, as these can leave an area unsterilised, which can potentially cause bacteria to grow.

Steam sterilisers

Steam sterilising is a quick and efficient method, but is expensive, and once the unit has been opened the bottles need to be prepared within a short period of time, as opening the steriliser allows the potential for bacteria to start to develop. There is also a risk of scalding from the release of steam if the unit is opened while still very hot, so great care must be taken. Steam sterilisers usually hold six or eight bottles at a time. They are ready for use within approximately 12–15 minutes from switching on the unit (see Figure 4.3).

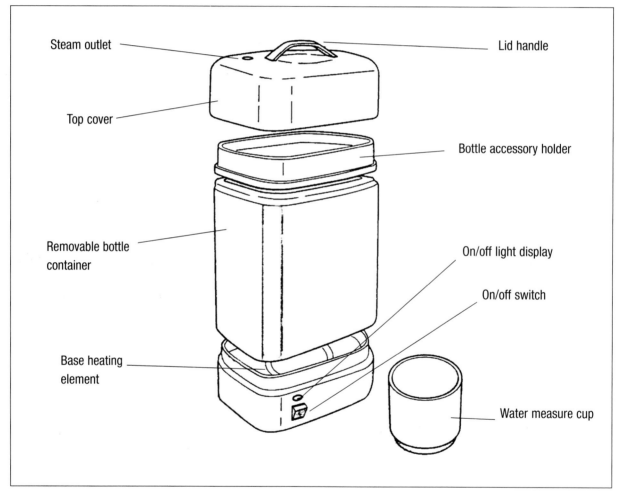

Figure 4.3   A steam steriliser unit

Microwave sterilisers

The microwave method works on the same principle as the steam steriliser method. The sterilising containers fit inside the microwave and usually only hold four bottles, but the method is quick (see Figure 4.4).

Points to remember

★ Metal objects MUST NOT be placed in a microwave steriliser.
★ Do not reheat milk in bottles in a microwave, as hot spots can occur, which could burn the infant.

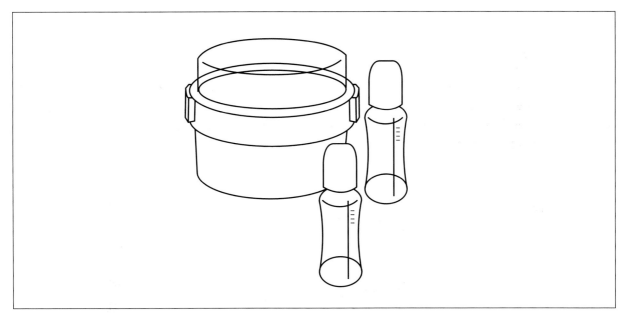

Figure 4.4 A microwave steriliser unit

Boiling method

Boiling feeding equipment is a cheap option, but is no longer a popular choice. The potential for accidents due to the use of large quantities of boiling water is high. However, it is an option when no other form of sterilising is available. It only takes ten minutes of boiling time to be ready. All equipment must be fully submerged, as with the cold water method.

Weaning

From about four months onwards (and usually by six months), babies begin to be less satisfied with what they receive from breast or formula milk and it becomes appropriate to introduce them to solid food. This transition is called 'mixed feeding', or 'weaning'. Breast and formula milks do not have sufficient iron for continued healthy development, and prolonged (exclusive) milk feeding will not provide enough of this important mineral to support a growing infant's development. Up to four months of age, babies retain sufficient stocks of iron taken from their mother during pregnancy, and below four months their digestive system is not usually mature enough to cope with the components of solid food.

Babies grow at their fastest rate during their first year and it is important that they are given a healthy and varied diet. This means a good balance of calcium, protein, carbohydrates and fats, together with a range of vitamins and minerals.

The four main food groups are:

● **Proteins**, which help growth, development and tissue repair
● **Carbohydrates**, which provide energy
● **Vitamins, minerals and fibre**, for general good health and the prevention of illness
● **Dairy products**, which are high in calcium, enhancing and maintaining bones and teeth.

Fats and oils are higher energy-giving foods which are also essential to children, but should be consumed sparingly by adults (see Figure 4.5).

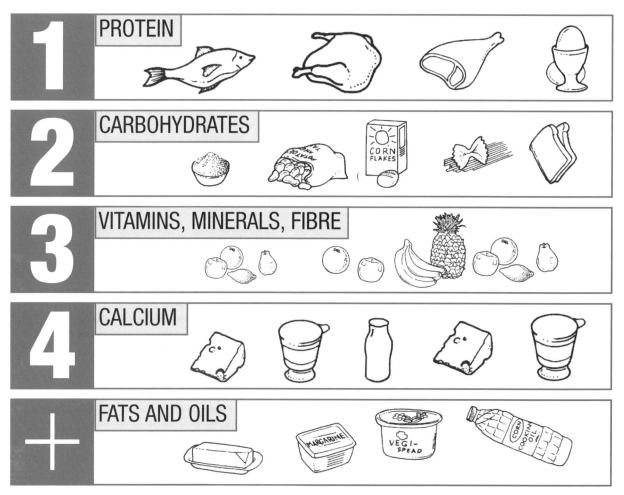

Figure 4.5 Food groups: the essential nutrients

Points to remember

★ Milk remains an important part of a baby's diet until he is at least a year old.
★ A subsidiary aim of weaning is to introduce babies to a variety of textures, tastes and experiences and to integrate them fully into family mealtimes.
★ It is important that you do not introduce weaning (or a new food) when a baby is unwell or tired.
★ Offering half of the milk feed before the solids and half afterwards works well for most babies, but all babies are different and they will soon indicate their individual preferences.

Weaning should be a happy experience for both carer and child, encouraging the infant to explore new tastes, gradually introducing them over a period of time. It should not be a situation of stress or tension. At times it can be difficult to get a baby interested in trying to take solids from a spoon, but it is important to keep on offering it without worrying about regular refusals. Initially the baby will still be having full milk feeds and will therefore not be losing out nutritionally, and every baby gets there in the end.

As the intake of solid food increases, the milk feeds will decrease until the baby is having sufficient solid food at a 'mealtime' to be satisfied with a drink of water to accompany it. Table 4.3 (page 128) gives an example programme for weaning a baby.

Weaning is an important part of development, both socially and physically. It is not usually beneficial to hold back the start of weaning for any length of time, even if the infant seems content with milk feeds. Research conducted at Bristol University in the early 1990s has shown that babies who are not introduced to mashed (rather than puréed) food by ten months of age are likely to be fussier eaters later on in their lives.

Points to remember

★ Mealtimes should be a pleasure, not a battle.
★ Always make gradual changes to the consistency of foods.
★ Only offer one new food or new consistency at a time.
★ Only offer new foods when the infant is well and content.
★ Introduce a new food alongside a familiar food, to ensure that at least something is eaten.
★ Feeding can be messy, so it should take place in a suitable environment.
★ Babies need to try to feed themselves in order to learn.
★ Happy mealtimes will encourage a positive attitude to food and eating later on.

Encouraging feeding independence

Babies enjoy trying to feed themselves. Most can cope with finger foods from about eight months onwards. Suitable foods include rusks, fingers of soft bread, pieces of pear and slices of banana. When an infant shows interest in trying to handle the spoon, give him a spare one. You will then remain in control of the feeding process, while satisfying his curiosity and allowing his skills to develop.

Physical care

Skin care

Research has shown how seriously the human skin can be damaged by the sun's rays, and babies and toddlers should never be exposed to the sun for more than a very short period of time. Babies should be kept in the shade whenever possible (always be aware of how the sun moves round during the day), and outdoor play in sunny areas should be restricted, particularly around midday when the sun is at its highest point.

Babies and toddlers should always wear hats, and sunscreen creams or lotions should be used as directed by the manufacturer. In an early years setting, there should

Table 4.3 Suggested dietary guidelines regarding weaning (Reproduced with the permission of Nelson Thornes Ltd, from *A Practical Guide to Working with Babies* (3rd edn) – Dare & O'Donovan – ISBN 0 7487 7349 5, first published 2003)

Age/months	4 months	4½ months	5–6 months	6–7 months	7–8 months	9–12 months
On waking	Breast- or bottle-feed	Breast- or bottle-feed	Breast- or bottle-feed	Breast- or bottle-feed	Breast- or bottle-feed	Breast- or bottle-feed/cup
Breakfast	1–2 tsp baby rice mixed with milk from feed or with water; breast- or bottle-feed	2 tsp baby rice mixed with milk from feed or with water; breast- or bottle-feed	Baby rice or cereal mixed with milk from feed or with water or puréed banana; breast- or bottle-feed	Cereal mixed with milk from feed or water; fruit, toast fingers spread with unsalted butter	Cereal, fish or fruit; toast fingers; milk	Cereal and milk; fish, yoghurt or fruit; toast and milk
Lunch	Breast- or bottle-feed	1–2 tsp puréed or sieved vegetables or vegetables and chicken; breast- or bottle-feed	Puréed or sieved meat or fish and vegetables, or proprietary food; followed by 2 tsp puréed fruit or prepared baby dessert; drink of cooled boiled water or well-diluted juice (from cup)	Finely minced meat or mashed fish, with mashed vegetables; mashed banana or stewed fruit or milk pudding; drink or cooled boiled water of well-diluted juice in a cup	Mashed fish, minced meat or cheese with vegetables; milk pudding or stewed fruit; drink	Well-chopped meat, liver or fish or cheese with mashed vegetables; milk pudding or fruit fingers; drink
Tea	Breast- or bottle-feed	Breast- or bottle-feed	Puréed fruit or baby dessert; breast- or bottle-feed	Toast with cheese or savoury spread; breast- or bottle-feed	Bread and butter sandwiches with savoury spread or seedless jam; sponge finger or biscuit; milk drink	Fish, cheese or pasta; sandwiches with savoury spread; fruit; milk drink
Late evening	Breast- or bottle-feed	Breast- or bottle-feed	Breast- or bottle-feed if necessary			

be a policy regarding the application of sunscreens, with written parental permission being obtained before staff apply cream to any child.

All sunscreen products for children and babies should be of the highest factor, or be a total sun block.

Hair care

Care of a child's hair is needed to prevent infestation from headlice and to encourage good grooming in the future. Cultural practices will differ: Muslim babies will have their heads shaved within 40 days of birth as part of their cultural tradition, and many Caribbean parents tradition-ally weave and plait their babies' hair at a very early age.

Not all babies like the sensation of water in their eyes, and washing their hair can be traumatic at times. Hair washing products should always be 'non-stinging' to the eyes, and hair rings can be used to prevent water from reaching the eyes. Simple precautions like these make for a happier bathtime.

Dental care

Good dental health care is important, and the brushing of a baby's teeth should start as soon as the first ones arrive, and definitely when a baby has corresponding teeth top and bottom (see Figure 4.6 for an illustration of teeth formation within infants). Soft baby toothbrushes are avail-able which are specially designed for the delicate gums and first teeth. Their regular use will encourage the baby into a habit of good oral health care for the future. In an early years setting every baby should have his own toothbrush, which should be labelled and kept separately from the others.

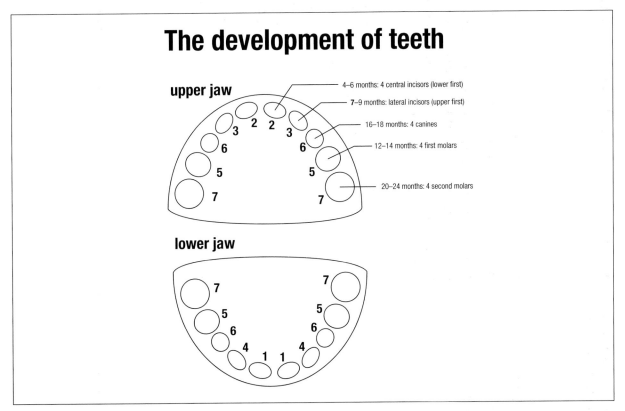

Figure 4.6 The development of teeth

Caring for a baby's feet

The feet of a baby are very delicate as the bones are still forming. It is therefore important that children are not given shoes before they are walking, to avoid any hindrance to their natural growth and development, which might lead to deformity. Socks, all-in-one suits and bootees should all have sufficient room for natural movement and growth.

When babies are ready to have their first pair of proper shoes it is important to have their feet measured and shoes fitted by a footcare specialist.

Babies' clothing

A suitable item of clothing for a baby is one that:

- is easy to put on and take off
- has room for the child to grow
- allows unrestricted movement
- is suitable for the time of year and temperature of the environment the child is in
- avoids cramping an infant's toes (for example, in all-in-one suits)
- is free from long ties or ribbons (to avoid choking)
- has no loose buttons or poppers (another choking hazard)
- avoids lacy designs or looped edgings on seams, which may catch small fingers
- is easy to wash and dry
- is made from natural materials such as cotton, which allows the baby's skin to breathe
- avoids fluffy materials or wools such as mohair, which can irritate noses, stick to hands and get into mouths
- is of a suitable length (i.e. not long enough to get caught when toddling or crawling)
- can be washed in non-biological powders to avoid reactions to the harsh detergents in many modern washing agents.

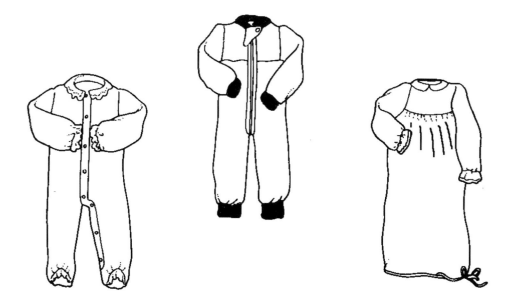

Point to remember

★ Babies are not able to control their body temperature and can easily become overheated. It is therefore better for babies to wear several layers of clothes that can be removed or replaced according to temperature, than one warmer layer which offers no opportunity for adjustment.

Maintaining correct body temperature

A constant room temperature is an important factor in looking after a baby, and any room where a baby spends a large amount of time should be a constant 20 °C (68 °F) day and night. Ideally, a room thermometer should be placed on the wall in the baby room of any early years setting and be checked regularly, adjusting the heating accordingly. Whenever possible, radiators should be controlled by thermostats, and fire or heater guards should be fitted where necessary.

Is the baby too warm?

You can check if a healthy baby is too warm or too cool by feeling the abdomen. If it feels warm and clammy then the infant is hotter than he should be. A slightly cool to touch abdomen is usual.

To cool a baby down simply remove a layer of clothing. This should be sufficient to keep the infant at a more comfortable temperature.

Overheating of babies is thought to be a contributory factor in sudden infant death syndrome (cot death), and recommendations are that babies should not be covered with layer upon layer of blankets. Just a sheet and two layers of blankets will normally be sufficient.

Duvets and baby nests are no longer recommended as they do not allow for temperature regulation. Cot bumpers are also advised against as they add extra warmth to a baby's cot and have the potential to cause suffocation.

Points to remember

★ A blanket folded in half counts as two layers.
★ Cool hands and feet do not automatically indicate a 'cold' baby. It should be remembered that the circulation of young babies is not as fully developed as in adults and older children, and many babies have cool extremities (hands and feet), especially before they have begun to crawl or toddle.
★ If a baby is unwell and appears to have a raised temperature, always check it with a thermometer and seek medical advice if you are concerned.

A high temperature (pyrexia)

The normal body temperature is between 36 °C (96.8 °F) and 37 °C (98.6 °F). A temperature above 37.5 °C (99.5 °F) indicates pyrexia (fever). The temperature of a young child can often be a useful indicator of the onset of illness and a raised temperature should never be ignored.

37.5 °C

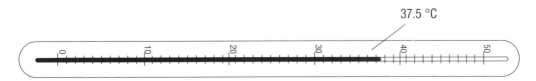

Check for overheating in the first instance by:

- removing a layer of clothing or a layer of bedding
- reducing the temperature of the room the baby or child is in, or taking the infant to another room
- sponging the baby or child with a cool flannel.

If pyrexia is suspected:

- take the child's temperature and make a note of it
- remove another layer of clothing or bedding
- sponge with a cool flannel
- offer plenty of fluids (water is ideal)
- use a fan to circulate cool air around the infant
- observe the child carefully, particularly if caring for a very young baby.

Febrile convulsions

Febrile convulsions can occur in some children when their temperature rises and involves loss of consciousness, flickering of eyes and general jitteriness. A child who has one febrile convulsion is more likely to have another. It does not, however, mean that he has developed epilepsy. The child should be placed in the recovery position when the convulsion is over while medical advice is sought. It is important that he receives reassurance and rest following a febrile convulsion.

> **Point to remember**
>
> ★ In an early years setting, parents should always be informed if their child has had a febrile convulsion, or has become unwell, even if the symptoms have disappearedand he appears well again by the time the child is collected.

Lighting

Natural light is important to adults as it helps avoid headaches and eye strain, and good lighting helps avoid accidents. This is particularly important when carrying babies or manoeuvring around young children.

Ventilation

Good ventilation lessens opportunities for cross-infection, but it should be remembered in early years settings that ventilation points need to be kept well cleaned, as they can easily attract dirt and a build up of bacteria.

 Checkpoint questions

1. Why do the care routines for babies need to alter as they get older?
2. What specific skin care might a black-skinned infant need?
3. In what order do a baby's teeth usually appear?

4. What is meant by the term 'topping and tailing'?
5. What should be the maximum temperature of a baby's bath?
6. What winding positions can you explain?
7. Why is breast milk considered best for a baby?
8. What is the difference between fore milk and hind milk?
9. What is 'safe practice' in caring for babies?
10. At what temperature should a baby's room be kept?
11. What body temperature indicates a fever?
12. What is a febrile convulsion?
13. From what age is paracetamol registered to be used to treat pyrexia?
14. Why is it important to add the correct ratio of formula to water when making up a bottle?
15. What is meant by 'possetting'?
16. What different types of sterilising methods can you describe?
17. What are the main points to consider when choosing clothes for babies?
18. Why are nut oils not recommended for use in baby massage?
19. What concerns have been raised regarding the use of talcum powder on babies?

Preventative care

The general health and safety of babies and toddlers should be upheld at all times. Their actions can often be unpredictable, with sudden uncoordinated movements. Careful handling and appropriate support of newborn infants is of utmost importance, and measures to prevent cross-infection need to be strictly adhered to, both in the home and in day care settings.

Supervision of infants in their prams is necessary, particularly if cats are around, or on hot days when a baby originally placed in shade can become exposed to the full rays of the sun as it moves round. Examples of safe practice with young babies are shown in Figure 4.7.

Security of babies in early years settings

In a care setting it is important that there is strict monitoring in place regarding who has access to babies. Usually there would be visual and/or audio monitoring of the sleep room, with staff members checking each infant regularly.

Standard measures preventing strangers gaining access to the setting should be established, and infants must only be handed over to the persons specified in advance to the setting by their main carer.

Good personal hygiene

The personal hygiene of all those working with babies and toddlers is important. Maintaining good levels of hygiene helps to prevent cross-infection and involves the following steps:

- washing hands regularly throughout the day
- washing hands before all food preparation
- washing hands after any activity that has the potential for bacteria (e.g. nappy changing, using the toilet, coughing, sneezing, nose blowing)
- regular use of antibacterial soaps

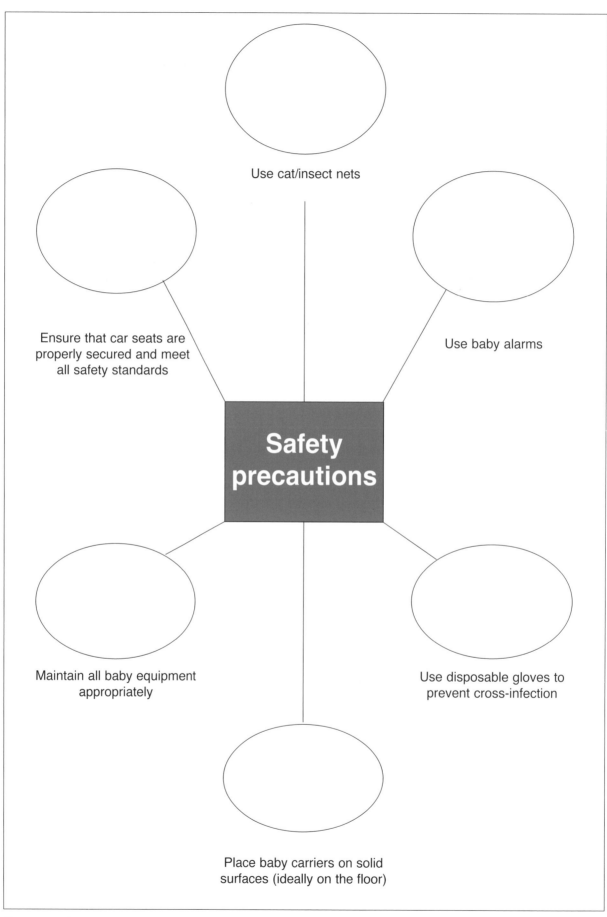

Figure 4.7 Safe practice with young babies

- keeping nails clean and short
- keeping cuts and sores covered
- using disposable gloves (in early years settings) when handling body fluids
- keeping hair tied back
- wearing clean clothing and/or overalls.

Safety

Toddlers face many potential hazards as they do not understand fear, or recognise danger. This makes them vulnerable. Toddlers' interest and inquisitiveness regularly exceed their physical strength, judgement and ability, and they place themselves in hazardous situations. This is why constant supervision is so important. Table 4.4 sets out some of the key safety measures linked to the development of babies and toddlers which can be taken to help prevent accidents occurring in the early years.

Table 4.4 Safe practice with babies and toddlers

Developmental stage	Safety measures
As a newborn infant	<ul><li>Change the baby on a safe surface</li><li>Cover pram etc. with a cat/insect net</li><li>Ensure that all baby carriers (e.g. Moses basket, carry-cot, etc.) are sturdy and conform to current safety standards</li><li>Use a suitable mattress for the baby's cot, ensuring that it is the correct size and conforms to current safety standards</li><li>Fit an appropriate (rear-facing) car seat.</li><li>AVOID cot bumpers, quilts and duvets. These have been linked to the overheating of young babies, which is thought to contribute to cot death</li></ul>
Once the baby can sit up	<ul><li>Be aware of new areas that can be reached by the baby</li><li>Flexes should be kept out of reach</li><li>Hot food should not be placed in front of the infant, in case he topples onto it</li><li>Attach harnesses to chairs, prams and strollers</li><li>Do not change the baby's car seat round (from rear- to forward-facing) until the correct weight has been reached (as indicated by the manufacturers)</li></ul>

Table 4.4 Safe practice with babies and toddlers (continued)

Developmental stage	Safety measures
Once the baby can crawl	• Play pens can be useful • Fire guards prevent babies accessing hearths • Use electric socket covers • A video guard can be attached to the video player to stop hands/arms getting stuck and to prevent objects from being 'posted' through the flap • Install safety gates at the top and bottom of stairs, and possibly across the kitchen door • Toilet lid catches can be useful • Secure all trailing leads from electrical equipment or similar • Protect sharp corners with transparent covers • Place safety glass (or a special safety film) in all full-length glass doors • Remove overhanging table cloths and ensure that hot drinks are out of the baby's reach • Keep cleaning fluids up high, preferably shut away out of sight • Be aware of pet food and pet water bowls • Remove loose carpet fibres (these can cause choking if swallowed) • Cover garden ponds with strong netting
When the baby is standing, climbing or toddling	• Cooker bars help to protect from saucepan spills • Keep pan handles turned inwards at all times • A fridge lock may be needed • Fit catches on windows, doors and drawers • Place safety glass (or special safety film) in glass doors, low windows, and on glass coffee tables

Toy safety for babies and toddlers

All toys should be made to a recognised safety standard. The chart in Table 4.5 gives an up-to-date range of safety marks.

Table 4.5 Safety marks (from Green 2002: 125)

Mark	Name	Meaning
	BSI Kitemark	Indicates a product has met a British Safety Standard and has been independently tested
	Lion Mark	Indicates adherence to the British Toy and Hobby Association Code of Practice and ensures a product is safe and conforms to all relevant safety information
	Age Warning	Indicates: 'Warning – do not give the toy to children less than 3 years, nor allow them to play with it' Details of the hazard, e.g. small parts, will be near the symbol or with the instructions
	BEAB Mark of the British Electrotechnical Approvals Board	Indicates that electrical appliances carrying this mark meet a national safety standard
	BSI Safety Mark on gas appliances, light fittings and power tools	Indicates the product has been made and tested to a specific safety standard in accordance with the British Standards Institute
	Safety Mark on upholstered furniture	Indicates upholstery materials and fillings have passed the furniture cigarette and match tests – a lighted cigarette or match applied to the material will not cause the article to burst into flames
	Low Flammability labels	Children's pyjamas, bathrobes made from 100% Terry towelling and clothes for babies up to 3 months old must carry a label showing whether or not the garment has passed the Low Flammability Test. Either of these two labels is acceptable. Always look for these labels when choosing such garments
	Keep Away From Fire label	Indicates the garment is not slow burning and has probably not passed the Low Flammability Test. Great care must be taken anywhere near a fire or flame

Safety in the home

The following general safety points should be followed in the home when babies and toddlers are present:

- smoke alarms should be installed
- safety mats should be placed in baths to stop the child from slipping
- slam stoppers can be fitted on doors, to prevent fingers being trapped
- razors, chemicals and medicines should be kept locked away securely

- cold water should always be added to baths before hot
- toys should be checked regularly to ensure they are intact, undamaged and clean.

Immunisation

Immunisation protects children against certain illnesses, and also helps to prevent infection passing on to children with a suppressed immune system who may not be able to have the vaccine themselves.

There are various different types of immunity:

- **active and natural immunity**, where the child builds his own immunity following an illness (e.g. as with chickenpox)
- **passive and natural immunity**, where antibodies from the mother have crossed the placenta or have been passed on through breast milk and protect a newborn infant
- **passive and acquired immunity**, obtained through an immunisation injection (e.g. as with Meningitis C)
- **active and acquired immunity**, through specifically being given a controlled amount of a live vaccine (e.g. as with Polio, which is given on a spoon)
- **herd immunity**, where a sufficiently high enough proportion of society are immunised (the figure for this is usually around 90%), enabling the remaining 10% of the population to remain free from the illness.

In some cases, siblings and others in close contact with a child with suppressed immunity may be given a special non-live version of a (usually) live vaccine to ensure that they do not accidentally pass any trace of the (live) vaccine on to the infant.

The recommended immunisation programme is set out in Table 4.6.

Table 4.6 The recommended immunisation programme

Age	Type of immunisation	Method of immunisation
At two months	HiB (Haemophilias influenzae type B) with Meningitis C	1 injection
	Diphtheria, Whooping cough and Tetanus	1 injection
	Polio	Given orally
At three months	HiB with Meningitis C	1 injection
	Diphtheria, Whooping cough and Tetanus	1 injection
	Polio	Given orally
At four months	HiB with Meningitis C	1 injection
	Diphtheria, Whooping cough and Tetanus	1 injection
	Polio	Given orally
Between 12 and 15 months	MMR (Measles, Mumps and Rubella)	1 injection
Between 3 and 5 years (the pre-school booster)	Diphtheria and Tetanus	1 injection
	MMR booster	1 injection
	Polio	Given orally
Between 11 and 14 years	BCG (Bacillus Calmette-Guerin) vaccine (this protects against Tuberculosis)	1 injection
Between 15 and 18 years	Diphtheria and Tetanus	1 injection
	Polio	Given orally

Links to Jasmine

Jasmine has had all the recommended immunisations for a child of her age. She suffered a high temperature following her first immunisations at two months, so she was given paediatric paracetamol (agreed with her GP) in advance of the next two immunisations. This prevented any change in her temperature.

Jasmine reached the age of 15 months at the height of the MMR debate in 2002, with its concerns about the vaccine's safety for children's health. After a great deal of thought and personal research on the part of her family, Jasmine was given the MMR vaccine as recommended by the primary health care team for her area.

Communication

One of our basic human instincts is to communicate with one another. Communication can be both verbal and non-verbal, and the way in which we respond to babies and toddlers through speech, gesture, facial expression and body language will give them messages and either encourage or discourage them to communicate with us in return.

As adults we encourage babies to share in a conversation with us, asking them questions, pausing for them to respond either verbally or with their bodies, and then making reaffirming comments. This is all part of what is called 'pre-verbal communication'. The encouragement and welcoming responses of the adult encourage the baby to vocalise further, enhancing his ability to communicate with the adult concerned and with others. Another term used to describe this is 'turn-taking'.

Motherese

Motherese is what is often referred to as 'baby talk'. Motherese speech is distinctive from normal speech between adults in that it:

- has a higher pitch than the speech that used with other adults
- is slower, with simplified words and phrases usually being used
- includes frequent pauses, to facilitate turn-taking between infant and adult.

Adults communicate with babies through:

- eye contact during breast- or bottle-feeding
- turn-taking vocally or visually
- initiating 'conversations' with babies during play
- responding to their cries
- recognising the needs of babies through their body language or facial expression
- encouraging them to vocalise
- showing appreciation of their vocalising
- giving praise
- calling to them when out of their visual range
- stimulating them through sound
- stimulating them with visual objects.

Baby massage

Baby massage is a form of communication which is very intimate. It is a popular and important means of communication between a parent and baby, as it enhances the parent's understanding of his or her baby's needs. Baby massage involves eye contact, touch, smiling and other pleasurable facial expressions, and enhances the interaction between parent and baby.

> **Point to remember**
>
> ★ Baby massage oils should not contain any traces of nuts, as this has been known to cause an allergic reaction in some infants.

Stimulating play

Babies and young children are stimulated by all that they see around them and through the multitude of experiences that they enjoy and are challenged by. This includes their toys. Learning through play is enhanced by the provision of a range of resources to stimulate all of the senses.

Stages of play

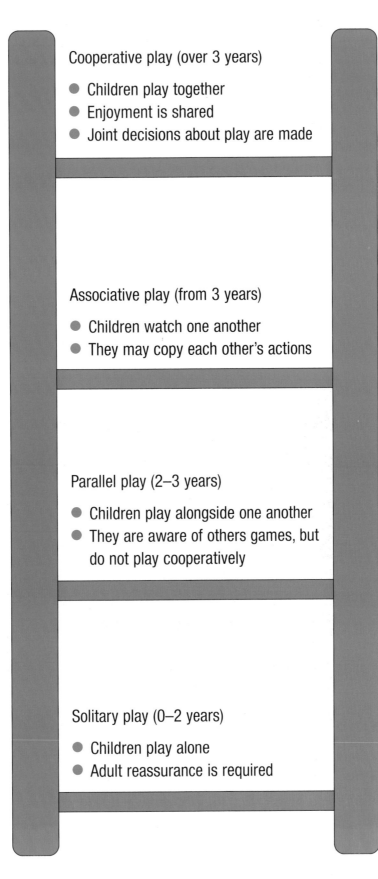

Cooperative play (over 3 years)

- Children play together
- Enjoyment is shared
- Joint decisions about play are made

Associative play (from 3 years)

- Children watch one another
- They may copy each other's actions

Parallel play (2–3 years)

- Children play alongside one another
- They are aware of others games, but do not play cooperatively

Solitary play (0–2 years)

- Children play alone
- Adult reassurance is required

Figure 4.8 The play stages ladder

The ladder in Figure 4.8 illustrates clearly how social play develops stage by stage. A child moves from the initial solitary actions of a toddler absorbed in his own world, up the steps of the play 'ladder' to the complexity of games involving rules that we see being played in the playgrounds of primary schools. This ability to cooperate with other children is dependent on both the maturity (and therefore the stage of development) of individual children, and the opportunities and experiences that have been provided for them.

- Solitary play
  The first stage of play is known as 'solitary play'. The child plays contentedly on his own, but still needs the reassurance of a familiar adult being close by. This play is typically seen up to the age of two years. Imitation is often evident, demonstrating the child's understanding of the actions of other people within his world. An example of solitary imitative play would be a child briefly putting a cup to the mouth of a doll or teddy. At the age of two Jasmine fits into the solitary play category.

- Parallel play
  The second stage in play is known as 'parallel play' because the child begins to enjoy playing alongside, but not actually with, another child or small group of children. The children rarely acknowledge one another at this stage, and make no reference to what the other is doing. This is true parallel play, with one child playing parallel to the other. It can usually be seen to develop between the ages of two and three years.

- Associative (looking on) play
  This next stage in social play sees the child beginning to watch the actions of others, enjoying their play from a short distance away. The child is not as yet ready to actually play with other children, but learns a great deal from observing them. This stage of play is typically seen between the ages of three and four years.

- Cooperative play
  By around four years of age most children are ready to play cooperatively with others. There are two kinds of cooperative play:
  1. *Simple cooperative (joining-in) play*: this begins in an uncomplicated manner. It involves the shared enjoyment of a similar activity. An example of this would be a group of children all playing with a construction set together. They have no rules to follow and there are no restrictions on what they do. It is simply a pleasurable play experience to be shared with others, chatting about what they are doing together as they go along.

  2. *Complex cooperative play*: this most advanced stage in the development of play involves the children interacting as a group. This could be through their involvement in the physical cooperation needed to complete a joint task, or within play which has complex rules, involving the taking on of agreed (though possibly evolving) roles.

Complex cooperative play

Stimulating toys

In the commercially led world of today, there are toys to stimulate every sense, and many people do not think of providing stimulation through ordinary household items. Providing that objects from around the house are clean, safe (no sharp edges) and do not involve small pieces (that could be swallowed or put up noses), they can make very satisfactory play materials.

This section of the book takes the reader through a selection of Jasmine's own toys, both home produced and commercially bought, highlighting how they have stimulated and delighted her at various stages of development (from birth, as a growing baby, and as a toddler). Jasmine's play has followed a pattern typical of many babies and toddlers, and therefore provides a good example of how play develops. Most of the toys have been photographed, but some are simply described.

Jasmine's toys have been thoughtfully selected by her family to provide an all-round sensory experience for her. At times her play with the same toy at a later date has also been referred to. There are many different varieties of toys illustrated and described here, produced by a range of different companies. There is no intention to promote or avoid any particular company or manufacturer. Choices were made at the time purely on the personal preference of the purchaser.

From birth

The traditional toy of the newborn infant is the rattle. Jasmine had a variety of these made from various materials. She had a mixture of hard plastic and soft pliable plastic rattles containing bells and other types of 'fillings' designed to produce different noises. She had rattles made entirely, or in part, of materials such as satin, corduroy and towelling, which often contained safely enclosed bits of polythene (excellent for scrunching), squeakers or multiple 'bits' that would cascade when tipped.

The bright colours of each item stimulated Jasmine visually, while the textures stimulated her orally and appealed to her sense of touch. The sounds produced by the rattles encouraged her to listen intently.

From just a few weeks of age Jasmine was seen to clearly enjoy being stroked with silk scarves and satin ribbons. As she lay on a blanket or in her basket, these would be slowly and gently pulled across her face and hands. She would always turn towards them and use her tongue to increase her ability to sense them. At times her hands reached out to grasp them, again enabling her to experience them through sight, touch and oral means.

Jasmine loved her animal mobile, which included a lion with a very prominent face (see the photographs of this on page 40). Of all the creatures on the mobile, she was fascinated by this animal in particular, and her eyes followed him as it went around her. She laughed at the lion and 'talked' to him directly.

Jasmine's baby gym kept her amused for considerable lengths of time. Her arms would at first touch items by accident, but these soon became purposeful movements as she realised her activities would be rewarded with actions or sounds, as well as visual pleasure. As time went on, Jasmine also used her feet to 'move' the items.

As a growing baby

Once Jasmine was able to lift her head securely when prone (on her tummy) she enjoyed holding items that gave instant sensory rewards (e.g. soft toys, rainmakers and rattles).

As soon as she was able to sit propped up she also enjoyed playing with her carousel of penguins, attempting to pat the handle with her hands, but not managing to press it down until much later on. Again, a mixture of vision, sound, texture and oral stimulation was being experienced here.

Once Jasmine could sit securely, her mother made her a treasure basket. This is a wicker basket filled with a variety of natural (safe) objects. Ideally, the treasure basket is explored by the infant without adult intervention, but supervision is of course required.

The selected objects in Jasmine's treasure basket were as follows:

- a large wooden doorknob
- several smooth and lumpy stones
- four large shells of different textures and shapes (no sharp edges)
- a large pine cone (care is needed to ensure there are no loose seeds)

- a metal spoon
- a triple-layered muslin bag of lavender (ensure the lavender is well secured inside)
- a small round tin
- a short piece of rope (with ends well sealed)
- an orange, which needs to be replaced regularly (not pictured)
- a natural sponge (not pictured)

Jasmine spent considerable lengths of time exploring her treasure basket. She selected and handled the items one by one, turning them over and over, and putting them to her mouth to explore them with her tongue and lips. The emphasis of a treasure basket is on natural materials and therefore no man-made materials would usually be included.

- Teething toys
Once infants start to teethe, the discomfort of the erupting teeth can be eased by providing them with textures on which to bite. These are often made of hard or textured (knobbly) plastic. Some are filled with water and can be cooled in the refrigerator to help relieve hot gums.

  Jasmine's favourite was her teething bunny (Posibunny). His knobbly ears were well chewed during days when Jasmine was experiencing some discomfort, and she was clearly attracted by his appealing face, his scrunchy feet (lovely to handle and listen to) and the mirror on his tummy, which she would look into and wonder at (babies of this age do not recognise themselves).

- Home-produced toys
Jasmine has a range of home-produced toys. 'Happy spoon' has been a real favourite of hers. She always smiles at him whenever she sees him, and he always seems to be able to cheer her up if she has been crying. He is simply a wooden spoon with a happy face on one side and a sad face on the other (drawn in indelible ink). Jasmine will always stare at the sad face if shown it, but smiles instantly when it is turned to the happy face. His firm texture has also proved to be of use during teething!

  Other home-produced items include plastic drinks bottles filled with various cooking ingredients (red lentils, sunflower seeds, tapioca). As a young baby Jasmine liked to knock these over, or roll them around the floor to obtain the sounds, and enjoyed the excitement of shaking them. As this book goes to press, Jasmine still enjoys these make-shift musical instruments, loving the variety of sounds she can get by shaking each bottle, either gently, vigorously, up and down, or from side to side. She also likes to compare the sounds made by each bottle. It is important to ensure that bottles like these are well sealed and checked regularly.

  When a toddler has reached the crawling stage, having a variety of bright stimulating toys encourages the infant to move towards them and to explore their colour, shape, sound and texture.

Large parcel rolls make wonderful moving toys and were chased enthusiastically by Jasmine once she could crawl. As a toddler she played a very social game by rolling them to and fro with an adult. Wooden and plastic cotton reels also provided her with another pleasurable experience. When tied up loosely with a brightly coloured boot lace, they were easy for her to hold, giving her tactile, aural and visual stimulation. As an 'over two' she now threads them with increasing skill.

'Worm' was made from the leg of an old pair of tights. His simple (embroidered on) face held Jasmine's attention for long periods at a time. He chased, captured and tickled her (with a little help from an adult), which she loved. As a young toddler she would put Worm on her own arm and be very pleased with herself. As a two-year-old (with Worm on her arm) she now chases, captures and tickles other people.

- Soft toys
  All babies and young children love soft toys, and Jasmine is no exception. She has a huge variety to choose from. One that has remained a firm favourite is 'Pussy cat'. Jasmine tucks him under her chin and 'loves' him, saying 'Ahhh'. She is always pleased to see him and at the age of two calls him 'Pussel Tat'!

- Books for babies
  It is never too early to introduce babies to books as they can be visually stimulated by the bright colours and bold designs on board, cloth or wooden books from birth.

As babies develop, they enjoy textured books which offer opportunities to 'touch and feel' teddies' paws and ears, dogs' tummies, cats' tails and so on. Providing bright, durable books at a very early age stimulates children's interest in books, and helps them develop the skills they need to turn pages more carefully at a later stage.

● Bath toys

Bath toys do not need to be commercial or expensive. Plastic household bowls or storage containers (with or without lids) are ideal for tipping and pouring, and can be handy for rinsing. Clean yoghurt pots can be threaded together to make a 'bath train', and empty squeezy bubble bath bottles can be cleaned thoroughly then filled with warm water so that the child can squeeze and squirt them.

● Hand–eye coordination

The development of hand–eye coordination is promoted by activities that involve building and precise manipulative skills. Jasmine particularly enjoyed her building bricks and stacking beakers. She also had a wooden person that was made by placing one part of the body on top of the next, and a set of stacking rings, which were built around a central pole.

As a young toddler

● **Toddlers are always active**

Jasmine has had a lovely range of active toys to stimulate balance, gross motor skills, and a general sense of movement, spatial awareness and confidence in her own abilities.

Jasmine's parents bought her a ball pool for Christmas (she was almost two). She squirmed, jumped and dived among the balls, laughing and squealing with delight. She threw balls out and tried to catch those thrown on top of her by her family. The ball pool therefore contributed to the development of both gross and fine motor skills.

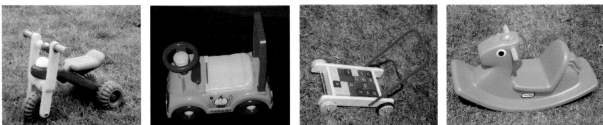

● **Fine motor skills**

As a young toddler Jasmine had a variety of toys that felt good to touch, made sounds and played music in response to an action, and involved a variety of different manipulative skills.

Among her favourites were shape sorters, which are excellent toys for this age group. Jasmine had a wooden drum-shaped sorter, which challenged her initially. If she could not get a piece through a designated hole she would simply post it through the top of a tissue box – very satisfying indeed! She also had a shape sorter car that played music and told you which shape you had 'posted' whenever you put one in correctly. Again, Jasmine avoided any sense of frustration by putting any 'difficult' shapes into the car through its back doors!

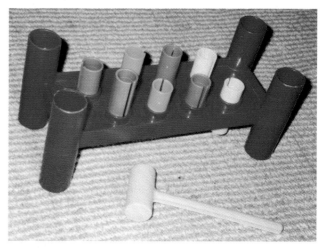

Jasmine also enjoyed using her hammer and pegs toy, gradually increasing the dexterous skills needed to knock the pegs all the way through the board.

Dexterity was also required to open up the garage doors of her three-car garage. Using her index finger, Jasmine pressed the catches to release the doors and then used a pincer grasp (finger and thumb) to open them right up. Toys of this kind can also help with early colour matching, as the cars correspond to the colours of each garage door, and Jasmine soon got into the habit of matching blue to blue, green to green, and red to red.

As a young toddler she adored playing with her dumper truck and used it well, first taking it onto the beach where it was used to transport sand, and then into the garden to move grass, daisies and fallen apples. At the age of two she now also transports her garden playhouse chalks (her 'dawdy talks') around in it.

Jasmine lives next to a farm and her first 'small world' play has been with farm animals (she has always loved the 'moo moos'). Handling the animals and trying to stand them securely on different surfaces uses fine motor skills – precise movements, careful manipulation and good hand–eye coordination.

Construction toys also help to develop these skills and come in many forms and sizes. It is important that children are given the resources most suitable for their age and stage of development. It is crucial that resources which include small pieces are withheld from children until they have stopped putting things in their mouth. It is also important to

remember the dangers of a younger sibling picking up small pieces if they are left lying around.

Jasmine's construction toys included the following:

- *Megablocks*: a set of these was given to Jasmine as her very first construction kit. They were lovely to handle, as the knobbly blocks can be manipulated simply and fit together firmly but easily. A toddler can make a satisfactory-looking construction quite quickly due to the large size of the blocks.

- *Duplo*: this is another set that has brought Jasmine an enormous amount of pleasure as a toddler. Again, the size and shape of the bricks makes them easy to handle. Play with a resource such as Duplo can be extended by the inclusion of farm animals, people, cars and other vehicles, including a Duplo train set. Between 2½ and 3 years old, the use of 'small world' toys (train sets, car mats, dolls' houses, zoos,

farms, etc.) becomes popular, and construction toys are gradually incorporated within the 'small world' play (as fences, walls, enclosures, etc.) to make highly complex floor-play games.

- *Sticklebricks*: simple to fit together, these bricks cling to one other on account of their 'brush-like' prongs. The sets tend to include small pieces, so are more suitable for the older toddler. As well as offering great scope for construction, Sticklebricks are visually stimulating and provide an interesting tactile experience.

One of the most important points to remember about construction toys is that children need enough of each type to be able to play with it in a satisfying way. The photographs shown above illustrate just part of Jasmine's supply of each type of resource.

- Concentration
  As toddlers get older their ability to concentrate increases. Having suitable toys and books available to them enables them to select and enjoy experiences on their own, as well as alongside an adult.

- Books for toddlers
  Toddlers love to read books and enjoy spending time looking through them with adults and being read to. Suitable books include picture books, alphabet-based books, books which group similar items together (e.g. insects, animals, garden items, etc.), and those that tell simple stories. Like most toddlers, Jasmine likes to hear the same books read over and over again, enjoying the familiarity of the experience and excitedly anticipating what will come next.

She has enjoyed books in which there is something specific to find (e.g. a duck) and those that contain simple messages which are relevant to her (e.g. using the potty (although the message doesn't seem to have quite got through yet!), and having a new baby in the family). One of her particular favourites was a book which featured a character with her name (*Jazzy in the Jungle* by Lucy Cousins, Walker Books 2002).

Although Jasmine's books sometimes needed repairing with sticky tape, as a result of frequent and often 'unskilled' handling, the constant availability of her books has helped Jasmine develop a strong interest in them, which should benefit her in the future.

- Imitation

  As toddlers develop, imitation of the adults they see around them becomes commonplace. Imitation is important in that it helps toddlers make sense of their world, giving them a chance to try new things out while they pretend to be someone else (e.g. a 'carer' of dolls and other belongings).

As an older toddler

- Creative activities

  Drawing and playdough are always favourite activities of older toddlers. Jasmine loves to colour with her crayons (her 'dawdy colours'). She has large chunky chalks outside in her garden playhouse (see photograph on page 97) and a blackboard on the inside wall, which has done nothing to discourage her from decorating the walls themselves!

- Puzzles

  From early on, simple play-tray puzzles help children with early matching skills and hand–eye coordination. Although it is important that the complexity of these increases, it is also crucial that children should not be overly challenged too soon, otherwise their interest will be overtaken by frustration. Matching skills and hand–eye coordination are both needed to support the development of reading and writing in the future.

- Colour matching

  Activities based on the Russian doll style, which involve ordering items according to certain characteristics, help children develop 'grading' skills (early maths) and enable them to classify things by size and colour (also early maths).

- More imitation

  As toddlers get older, more and more imitative play is seen. Jasmine loves cooking and making tea, and is particularly fond of dressing up. Hats are a favourite of hers, and she likes to wrap herself in a pretty sarong belonging to Mummy, or failing that a blanket.

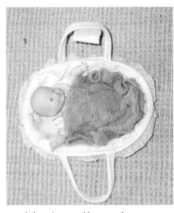

Doll play is a favourite game of hers too, and this was particularly encouraged by Jasmine's parents as they prepared her for the arrival of their new baby.

As this book goes to press, Jasmine continues to enjoy her doll play, imitating Mummy feeding her 'Beebee'. She likes to sort out items such as clothes pegs into colours and to line them up in rows. She has been provided with a large number of milk container tops (green, red and blue), collected over several months, for sorting and classifying, which again helps Jasmine with early understanding of maths principles.

> **Point to remember**
> ★ All children are different, and the toys with which they are provided should be suitable for the stage of development they have reached, and should stimulate them further in new and exciting ways.

The adult role

The most important resource for all children, helping to stimulate them in their play, is adult time. Each of us needs to take time to think through what is best for our children, to find time to play and talk with them. This way we provide them with the most stimulating start in life that we could possibly give them, and we also learn from them and enjoy their company all the more.

Jasmine has been, and continues to be, a wonderful playmate and companion for all the adults in her family. She will no doubt have plenty to teach baby Harry too.

Appendix: Answers to checkpoint questions

Chapter 1

Page 33

1. When a neonate is delivered he has many distinct features with regard to skin, eyes, senses and general appearance. These can include:

   - sleeping most of the time
   - lack of head control
   - a creamy white substance covering the body (vernix caseosa)
   - a soft downy hair called lanuga
   - fontanelles (posterior and anterior) which close over after a few weeks, and by around 18 months respectively
   - a flattened or misshapen head due to moulding during birth
   - the umbilical 'stump'
   - swelling or bruising, again due to the birth process
   - sticky eyes
   - uncoordinated eyes
   - eye colour which is not usually permanent
   - a flexed posture
   - poor circulation, often resulting in a bluish tinge to hands and feet
   - swollen genitalia, due to the mother's hormones crossing the placenta
   - slight vaginal blood loss in girls, again due to the transference of the mother's hormones
   - breasts of both boys and girls swollen and leaking a little milk, again due to the transference of the mother's hormones
   - black/green stools (faeces) initially
   - spots and rashes
   - peeling skin
   - neonatal jaundice
   - birthmarks at the time of delivery, or shortly after birth. Examples include: port wine marks (dark red patches, often on the face); the strawberry naevus (haemangioma) (raised patches); the 'stork bite' (often seen on eyelids, top of the nose, or back of the neck); Mongolian blue spots (dark marks found at the base of the spine on non-caucasian babies. They often look like bruises, and need mapping by health professionals to avoid mistaken concerns regarding abuse); CMNs (congenital melanocytic naevi) (large moles)
   - Reflexes such as: the blinking reflex; the rooting reflex; the sucking reflex; the palmar grasp; the plantar reflex; the stepping reflex; the moro reflex; the startle reflex; the asymmetric tonic neck reflex.

2. Explanations of primitive reflexes might include:

    * Blinking: the reaction to sudden lights, noises or movements in front of the infant's face.
    * Rooting: this is where the neonate turns his face towards the mother to locate the breast.
    * Sucking reflex: an infant will usually suck whatever touches his mouth, for example a clean finger.
    * Palmar grasp: an infant's response of grasping firmly whatever touches the palm of his hand. Gentle stroking of the back of the hand will usually release this.
    * Plantar reflex: touching the sole of an infant's foot with a finger will result in the flexing of the toes towards your finger.
    * Stepping reflex: the infant's foot responds to contact with a firm surface, resulting in a small 'step' being taken.
    * Moro reflex: a sudden movement of the neck is interpreted by the infant as falling. He throws out his arms with the hands open, and reclasps them over his chest.
    * Startle reflex: the infant throws out his arms at a sudden noise or movement, but the fists remain clenched.
    * Asymmetric tonic neck reflex: when the infant is turned to one side he will respond by straightening the arm and leg on the same side, while flexing the limbs opposite.

3. Vernix caseosa is a creamy white protective substance which covers the body of an infant in the later stages of pregnancy. It lubricates the skin and is usually seen on pre-term infants, and is often still present in full-term infants too.

4. The usual cause of neonatal jaundice is immature liver function and a subsequent rise in bilirubin levels (bilirubin is formed when red cells break down and the liver is unable to cope with its workload). If it is going to appear, it usually occurs around day three after birth. Earlier than three days can indicate liver disease or sepsis (both can be life threatening to the infant). Jaundice can occasionally be due to conditions such as galactosaemia, rubella virus, or cytomegalovirus.

5. The Apgar score measures five features of the newborn infant: heart rate; respiration; muscle tone; response to stimulation; colour.

6. The mother's hormones crossing the placenta can result in: swollen genitalia in both boys and girls; vaginal blood loss in girls; and swollen breasts, which may leak a little milk, in both boys and girls.

7. The birthmark which is usually only found on dark-skinned infants is the Mongolian blue spot. It is most commonly seen at the base of the spine. These marks are usually mapped by health professionals as they can look like bruises, potentially leading to concerns about physical abuse.

8. The anterior fontanelle closes over by 18 months, whereas the posterior fontanelle closes over within a few weeks of birth.

9. Babies born to black parents usually appear pale at birth as the skin pigmentation 'melanin' does not reach its full levels until later on.

10. The developing foetus can be affected by a range of factors, including: pre-conception issues such as the mother's diet, level of exercise, smoking, alcohol consumption and use of drugs (prescribed as well as recreational); genetic inheritance; infections experienced by the mother during pregnancy.

11. Folic acid is considered to be an important supplement for pregnant women as it contributes to the optimum development of the baby's central nervous system. Women are recommended to take folic acid before becoming pregnant and for the first 12 weeks of pregnancy to help prevent conditions such as spina bifida occurring.

12. Screening processes during pregnancy include:

  - routine blood tests to test for low iron levels, venereal disease and rubella (German measles). Low iron levels will be boosted by supplements, and women who are not immune to rubella will be advised to avoid contact with the virus during the early weeks of pregnancy.
  - an ultrasound scan is carried out as a routine test at 20 weeks of pregnancy. It measures the main bones, such as the femur (thigh bone), the head circumference and fluid levels, and carefully examines the heart chambers.
  - serum alpha-fetoprotein (SAFP) is a test to identify the possibility of spina bifida.
  - the triple blood test takes into consideration the mother's age and the SAFP test, together with measurements of human chorionic gonadotrophin (HCG) and placental hormones (oestrials). The combination of these tests gives an assessment of the risk that the foetus has Down's syndrome. It is offered to older mothers and to those thought to be at risk.
  - amniocentesis also checks for chromosome disorders such as Down's syndrome. It involves sampling the amniotic fluid, while linked to ultrasound, and is usually conducted between 16 and 18 weeks. It carries a slight risk of miscarriage.
  - chorionic villi sampling (CVS) involves removing a tiny amount of tissue directly from the placenta between 8 and 11 weeks. It also helps to identify a range of inherited disorders, and also carries a slight risk of miscarriage.

13. Centile charts are used to measure weight, height (length in babies), and head circumference. They indicate averages, and also the average ranges, within which 80 per cent of all infants are placed.

14. Amniocentesis is carried out by taking a sample of the amniotic fluid, usually between 16 and 18 weeks of pregnancy. Chorionic villi sampling involves the removal of a tiny amount of tissue directly from the placenta, usually between 8 and 11 weeks of pregnancy. Both are used to check for the possibility of abnormalities, and both procedures carry a risk of miscarriage, though amniocentesis carries a lesser risk.

15. A genetically inherited disorder is a disorder present from conception. It can be due to either autosomal recessive, autosomal dominant, or X-linked transference of a condition. A congenital disorder differs in that its origin is not from the gene bank of the parents.

16. 'Genotype' is the term used to describe the complete genetic inheritance of one person. 'Phenotype' refers to the visible arrangements of the characteristics that the person has inherited.

17. Foetal alcohol syndrome affects infants born to mothers who are alcoholics or very heavy drinkers. It causes developmental delay, deformities and learning difficulties.

18. The most common effect on an infant due to the mother smoking in pregnancy is low birthweight. There is a suggestion that it can also lead to a higher incidence of sudden infant death syndrome (also known as SIDs or cot death). Passive smoking is thought to contribute to respiratory problems in children as they get older.

19. 'Hypertonic' is the term used to explain that the infant's limbs have tension, whereas 'hypo-tonic' is the term used to explain that the neck is weak and there is no head control.

20. Vitamin K is given at birth to prevent the rare but exceedingly dangerous condition of neonatal haemorrhage. It can be administered either by mouth or by injection.

21. The introduction of formula feed to Jasmine during the first 24 hours ensured that her energy levels were kept up and she did not weaken. However, the regular 'topping up' through formula-feeding lessens the natural instinct of hunger and consequently the impetus to suck. This can cause a delay in the establishment of breast-feeding.

22. Jasmine was placed just below the 9th centile for weight, just above the 25th centile for head circumference, and on the 98th centile for length.

23. Babies can lose up to 10 per cent of their birth-weight without any concern from health professionals. Jasmine was slightly above this and her weight was therefore closely mon-itored.

24. The presence of menstrual blood and (in both boys and girls) swollen breasts is due to the mother's hormones crossing the placenta.

Chapter 2

Page 40

1. The social smile is usually seen by six weeks. Later than seven weeks can give rise to concern.

2. Gross motor skills are the physical skills which involve whole body movements.

3. Fine motor skills involve the development of hand and finger coordination, with infants gradually developing the ability to control their environment and the objects within it.

Page 45

1. Slow weight gain can be due medically to sucking difficulties, poor absorption, intolerance to formula milk, or illness. It can also be due socially to insufficient feeding, a poor mother-infant relationship, or poverty. Jasmine was breast-fed and sucked slowly and steadily. She was also very active when awake, with arms and legs constantly on the go. This was the reason attributed to her slow weight gain.

2. Infants do not usually roll over from supine to prone until they are four months old, often much later.

3. By three months infants usually show awareness of caring routines.

Page 47

1. Massage is a tactile experience, involving close contact with the carer. It plays an important part in the bonding process within many parent–child relationships as both parties are focusing fully on each other and making eye contact.

2. The triple immunisation protects against Diphtheria, Whooping cough and Tetanus.

3. HiB (Haemophilus influenzae type B) protects against a particular strain of meningitis that most commonly affects young infants.

Page 52

1. It is standard practice to refer a baby to his GP or a paediatrician if weight continues to cause concern, and infants are automatically referred if their weight crosses two centile lines in either direction.

2. The iron that was stored during pregnancy is used up by six months of age and there is a need for babies to receive iron within their diet. Between four and six months is the average age at which babies are introduced to solids, initially being offered smooth, puréed foods prior to the introduction of a variety of tastes and textures which help the baby to enjoy full family meals by the end of the first year.

3. It is recommended that babies avoid gluten (a protein found in wheat, barley, oats and rye) until at least six months of age as early introduction can trigger gluten intolerance (Coeliac disease). As Jasmine's grandmother is Coeliac, her parents refrained from introducing foods containing gluten for longer than average.

4. Toxocariasis can be contracted from the faeces of cats and dogs, so stringent handwashing is needed when handling pets and babies to lessen the possibility of cross-infection. A cat (or insect) net is necessary if a cat is likely to be moving around a sleeping baby, to avoid the risk of suffocation. Particular attention must be given to a baby when he starts to crawl, as items such as cat litter trays will be of great interest to him.

Page 54

1. A pseudo squint is not a real squint at all. Babies with a wide bridge to their nose (such as Jasmine) can occasionally appear to have one, and this can be confirmed by observing the baby in a bright light. If a distant object is reflected in both eyes in the same position, there is no squint. If the reflection is in a different position in each eye, a squint is present.

2. Earliest foods would include baby rice, soon to be followed by puréed fruit and vegetables (Jasmine particularly favoured banana). An example of a main meal could be puréed swede or turnip mixed with potato and lentils, followed by stewed fruit.

3. Babies of around six months are stimulated by all of their senses. They need safe, clean items that they can handle freely and take to the mouth. Jasmine enjoyed anything that gave her bright colours, movement or noise.

Page 58

1. There is no set age for commencing swimming. Some parents take their babies from just a few days old, others like to wait until the first immunisations have been given. It is very much a matter of personal choice. The main factors are to ensure the water is warm (sessions especially for parents and babies are best) and that the baby is in good health. It is important to remember that babies are not able to regulate their body temperature as adults do, and therefore they do not shiver to indicate that they are getting cold.

2. Legs and feet tend to be the strongest limbs, and the constant activity creates a backwards movement in young babies.

3. No, hand preference shown in young babies is not necessarily an indication for the future. Some babies will of course continue to show the same preference at a later age, but it is not a general indicator of left- or right-handedness.

4. Babies love pictures of other babies. Research has shown that they respond to faces more than any other pattern or shape, an early indication of the need for social interaction. Jasmine is no exception.

5. Ideal first finger foods would include slices of banana, fingers of lightly toasted bread, pieces of ripe pear, unsweetened rusks or baby rice cakes.

6. Babies begin to move from around six months of age, often backwards on their tummies (commando style). Traditional crawling occurs mostly from around eight months.

Page 60

1. Once weaning is well established and a baby is having three 'meals' a day (usually within two months of weaning commencing), cooled boiled water can be offered at the midday meal. Milk continues to be an important part of other meals throughout infancy.

2. As a baby becomes more mobile, appropriate safety measures to implement would include socket covers, fire guards, safety gates, and the removal of unsuitable items such as small objects and animal foods.

Page 62

1. A 'treasure basket' is a collection of objects that are made from natural materials. They need to be easy to handle and safe to explore, stimulating each of the infant's senses. Nothing in a treasure basket should be made of plastic or any other man-made material. Suitable objects include natural sponges, an orange, a wooden clothes peg, and a firm fir cone.

2. The pincer grasp is established when an infant can pick up tiny items between the index finger and thumb.

3. The term used to confirm that an infant has understanding that an object exists even when it cannot be seen is 'object permanence'.

Page 66

1. Some infants will copy an adult clapping from about nine months. By one year of age most infants will usually clap and also 'wave bye-bye' spontaneously.

2. The first teeth are usually the four front teeth (the central incisors). The lower ones usually appear first. The central incisors are normally followed by the four lateral incisors, the upper ones appearing before the lower ones. The first molars arrive from about one year onwards, with the canines at around 16 months and the second molars just before the second birthday.

Page 68

1. Most infants start to walk between 12 and 14 months.

2. From around seven months many babies become wary of people unfamiliar to them, clinging more to their main carer.

3. The term used to describe the positive responses given to Jasmine by her family is 'positive reinforcement'.

Page 70

1. There is no evidence that a baby-walker helps infants to walk earlier. They can in fact hinder walking as they can delay the natural process of gross motor skills development.

2. As walking becomes established, a push-along toy of some description is useful in offering the toddler support and helping to build confidence.

3. By one year old, infants should be enjoying full family meals. Most infants will now have moved on to cow's milk, unless they are still having breast-feeds morning and night. In families where Coeliac is present (as in Jasmine's) the infant can now gradually be introduced to foods containing gluten.

4. At one year old, babies are usually very sociable with people they know, but are still rather shy with strangers. They enjoy having other babies around, but only in a general way. They show no particular interest, as yet, in what others are doing.

Page 74

1. Shape sorters are excellent toys to encourage manipulative dexterity and hand–eye co-ordination, each shape being explored manually and positioned for 'posting'.

2. Babies can benefit from books from the earliest weeks of life, with bright clear pictures being positioned to attract their attention, and hard cover books given to them as their ability to hold objects develops. Sharing books with babies and toddlers is an important aspect of both social and cognitive development.

Page 76

1. At 14 months, play is still largely solitary. At this age toddlers would be expected to watch the actions of others and to enjoy the company of adults while still largely 'doing their own thing'.

2. Fruit is an important part of Jasmine's diet, providing vitamins, minerals and fibre. It is always better to offer fresh fruits and vegetables rather than cooked, as the cooking process diminishes the nutritional value of the food.

3. Toddlers need to be offered plenty of high energy foods such as cereals, pasta, breads and starchy vegetables, together with milk and dairy products for good teeth and bone development, and protein foods such as meats, pulses or fish (white or oily) to support growth.

4. Teething can be relieved by offering cooled teething rings (refrigerated in advance), hard objects that can be gnawed safely, and special gels to soothe the gums. At times, liquid paracetamol may help to relieve symptoms, but it should be remembered that paracetamol is not registered to be given to babies under the age of three months (should teething occur very early).

Page 78

1. As Jasmine positions the safety strap attached to her pushchair onto her toy or cup, waiting for the item to be secured, she is demonstrating understanding and memory (cognitive development), together with manipulative dexterity (physical development).

2. It is important for a child's shoes to be fitted properly as the bones in the foot are still forming, and feet can be damaged by cramped or ill-fitting footwear. Whenever possible, children's shoes should be made from natural materials to allow their feet to breathe, and there should be sufficient room for growth in shoes, slippers and socks. For babies and toddlers this also applies to all-in-one sleepsuits.

3. One of the main concerns regarding the MMR immunisation has been a suggested link between development of Autism and/or bowel disorders and the MMR vaccination. The subsequent drop in the numbers of children being immunised has raised concern regarding likely outbreaks of measles, mumps and rubella, and the ability to maintain control of these illnesses through herd immunity.

4. Through having pets at home children learn about their needs, how to treat them properly, and why it is important to respect them. This contributes to the development of consideration and care within a child's personality.

Page 82

1. A high level of supervision is extremely important in activity centres and soft play areas as young children are unable to assess their own limitations as their physical skills develop, and on account of the fact that they do not understand danger. Adults need to guide, supervise, and at times limit a child's activities to ensure safe enjoyment and progression.

2. Jasmine's attendance at her local soft play centre has enhanced her physical development through giving her increased opportunities to climb, balance, and scramble over, under and through objects with decreasing support levels from her mother. The safety surfaces allow for greater autonomy and ever-increasing physical confidence.

Page 83

1. It is a common stage in the development of toddlers to over-extend the use of a word. For example, all four-legged animals might be referred to as 'dogs'. In Jasmine's case, all birds were 'ducks'!

2. Jasmine shrunk back from the approaching shark in the zoo's underwater world because her sense of perception did not as yet take into account the glass barrier separating her from the contents of the tank.

3. From around the age of two years onwards children are usually beginning to dress themselves with some accuracy.

Page 85

1. Jasmine eats her meals better when listening to tapes or to the radio because she is concentrating on the music and eating with less focus on the food.

2. Toddlers of Jasmine's age love to return to the same books over and over again. It helps them consolidate their understanding of what they are seeing, with the adults reinforcing the names of objects for them.

3. Familiar items are an important aspect of all young children's lives. They offer an element of security within both their immediate and extended environment.

Page 91

1. Children of Jasmine's age like things to be in their 'correct' place because that is what they have observed and how they understand their world to be. For many children familiarity and routine form an important part of their security.

Page 93

1. The early stage of imitative play is very common at Jasmine's age and examples of this would usually be noted by an adult well into a child's third year, demonstrating how toddlers begin to make sense of their world by observation and experience.

2. Other examples of imitative play that Jasmine might display include cooking, shopping, dusting and similar day-to-day tasks.

3. From around the age of 20–24 months the second molars are usually erupting. However, Jasmine's tooth eruption pattern has been slower than in many children and she has only recently had her lower first molars arrive. She has not as yet had her canines either.

4. When encouraging children of Jasmine's age to help dress themselves, ideally the adult would allow them time to try to get the hang of it, give lots of praise for their efforts, and provide clothing items without complex fastenings.

5. Frustration in a toddler is best handled by offering help, while ensuring you are maintaining their involvement. At this stage in their development toddlers can visualise what they want to achieve, but often are not yet sufficiently well coordinated to achieve it.

6. Jasmine's developing language is likely to involve additional new words each week, with the increased use of two-word phrases.

Page 96

1 Jasmine's first drawing actions involve irregular side to side 'scribbles', with occasional firm dots.

2 When adults watch television alongside toddlers, they can help the children's development by talking to them about what they are seeing, and by making links to the toddlers' own experiences. It is also valuable as a social (shared) experience, demonstrating that the adult finds pleasure in the child's company.

3 By the age of two most children can say around 50 words, some of which are likely to be clearer than others.

Page 99

1. Many toddlers become temporarily obsessed with wearing or carrying certain items. Unless these items could cause them harm, there is no problem in the children taking them to bed. It is pointless to make an issue of something that does no harm to anyone.

2. Toddlers are extremely active, yet their balance and coordination are not always as advanced as their intentions. It is therefore important that safety surfaces are in place and sharp edges protected. Safety catches on doors and windows are crucial, and constant supervision is needed. Household items that could harm toddlers must be kept well out of reach, and medications, bleaches and chemicals should be safely locked away. This all helps minimise accidents.

3. At times, toddlers can find 'special' occasions overwhelming. Their routine has usually altered and the additional excitement of visitors, presents, balloons or party fun is often too much for them. Their sense of security lessens, and clinging, shyness and tears often follow.

4. Jasmine clearly recognised herself in the video she was imitating. Toddlers enjoy looking at pictures of other children, but are especially interested in pictures of themselves.

5. Introducing simple rules or boundaries to toddlers helps develop their understanding of the need to take other people or circumstances into consideration. In the earliest stages, it helps form practical routines, as with Jasmine swapping over her large toys. As she grows older clear boundaries will affirm her sense of security, as she will know her limitations within the home.

6. Bowel and bladder control can only take place once the child's nervous system is mature enough to enable him to recognise the associated feelings, and once his muscle control has developed sufficiently to support understanding. Between 18 months and two years most toddlers begin to make these associations and will indicate a need to use the potty, or that they have already 'been'.

7. Young toddlers develop the ability to initiate games with others; their actions, facial expressions, or vocalisations indicate the nature of the game. In this instance Jasmine was initiating hide and seek, letting her carers know that it was time to play through her actions and by calling out the words she wanted to hear them say.

8. Imitative play helps Jasmine make sense of her world. She can be different people and carry out different activities, practising and refining her skills for the future.

9. Tantrums are common at around two years old, but children of this age can usually be distracted from them quite easily. This becomes less easy when they reach two-and-a-half.

Chapter 3

Page 109

1. The main stages of language development are:
    *   non-verbal communication/expression
    *   speech-like noises
    *   controlling sounds, using mouth and tongue
    *   imitating sounds
    *   first words
    *   development of vocabulary
    *   putting words together to form simple phrases and sentences
    *   use of grammar
    *   use of meaning
    *   using language to develop other skills, for example early literacy.

2. By two years of age the average number of recognisable words is 50.

3. Object permanence is reached when a baby knows that an object exists even when it not there (or has been covered up).

4. Echolalia is a common linguistic phase in which children repeat the last word or sound they hear.

Chapter 4

Pages 132–3

1. Care routines for babies need to alter as they get older to accommodate their changing developmental needs. Aspects that need to change include: sleeping patterns; feeding times; amount of play time and stimulation; amount of rest and relaxation.

2.   Black-skinned babies are particularly prone to dry skin. The parents of many of the babies with this problem use cocoa butter rubbed into their skin to keep it moist.

3.

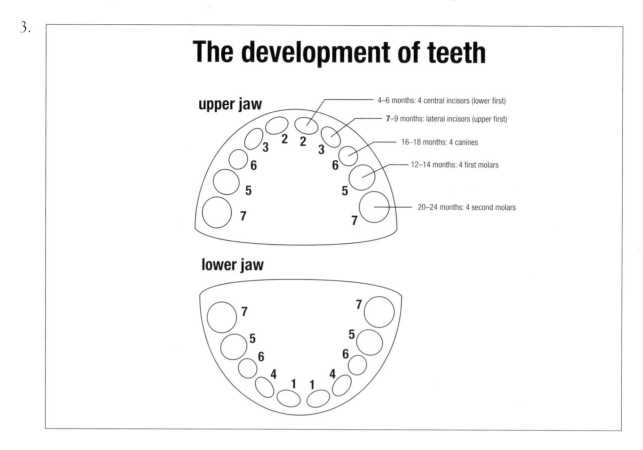

The development of teeth

upper jaw

- 4–6 months: 4 central incisors (lower first)
- **7–9 months**: lateral incisors (upper first)
- 16–18 months: 4 canines
- 12–14 months: 4 first molars
- 20–24 months: 4 second molars

lower jaw

4.   Topping and tailing involves washing the face, refreshing the top half of the body, and changing the nappy.

5.   The maximum temperature of a baby's bath should be 37 °C (98.6 °F). It should always be checked before the baby is lowered into it, preferably with a bath thermometer.

6.   Babies can be winded in several different ways (although often one way will suit a baby best). They mostly involve holding the baby upright to allow the air to 'rise'. Positions include:

- Sitting the baby forward so he is resting against your hand, while you rub or gently pat his back with your other hand.
- Placing the baby on your shoulder and rubbing or gently patting him.
- Resting the baby in a prone position (on his tummy) and rubbing his back (very young babies only).
- Laying the baby across your lap and rubbing his back.

7.   Breast milk is considered best for a baby as it contains protective substances that help to keep the newborn infant free from infection. It has a high protein content, which is particularly beneficial to pre-term infants. It is often called nature's 'designer food' and it adjusts to the needs of the infant as he grows. It provides the total nutritional needs of most infants for the first few months. The main benefits of breast-feeding are:

- it is the most natural food a child can be given
- the milk changes to meet the needs of the baby
- it is available on a supply and demand basis

- the colostrum-rich early milk is particularly high in protein
- it offers a degree of immunity to the newborn infant.

8. Lactation produces two stages of milk production. The fore milk satisfies the initial thirst and hunger of the infant, and the hind milk, which is the richer type of milk due to its higher fat content, offers longer-term satisfaction.

9. Safe practice when caring for young babies includes:
   - handling them carefully, offering full support
   - strictly adhering to preventative measures regarding cross-infection
   - careful supervision
   - the use of cat/insect nets
   - the use of baby alarms
   - ensuring that baby chairs, car seats, etc. are placed only on appropriate surfaces and are held in place securely
   - maintaining all baby equipment appropriately
   - ensuring that all equipment meets safety standards.

10. The room temperature for a baby should be a constant 20 °C (68 °F).

11. A potential fever involves a temperature above 37.5 °C (99.5 °F). Babies' extremities (hands and feet) often remain cold even when their overall body temperature is fine, due to their inability to regulate their temperature as well as adults and older children. It is therefore important that they are not 'over-wrapped'.

12. A febrile convulsion is where a baby has a raised temperature, together with loss of consciousness, flickering of the eyes, or general jitteriness.

13. Paracetamol is registered as suitable for treatment of pyrexia (high temperature) from over three months of age.

14. It is important to add the correct ratio of formula to water when making up an infant feed to prevent under- or over-feeding. Insufficient scoops of formula can lead to a hungry baby and poor weight gain. Heaped scoops of formula can lead to excessive weight gain and high levels of salt intake, possibly putting a strain on the immature kidneys.

15. The term 'possetting' refers to the small amount of milk that a baby regurgitates, often when being winded.

16. Infant feeding equipment can be sterilised in any of the following ways:
    - Cold water steriliser, using either a sterilising solution or a soluble sterilising tablet (both of these methods require the complete submergence of all items in the water and it takes 30 minutes for sterilisation to take place).
    - Steam sterilisers are quick to use, but once opened all items need to be used within a short amount of time
    - Microwaving works quickly and is similar to steam sterilising. Metal items cannot be included.
    - Boiling is no longer a popular choice due to the potential for accidents with using large amounts of boiling water. Items needs to be fully submerged in boiling water for at least ten minutes.

17. When choosing clothing for babies, it is important to ensure that:

    - there is room to grow
    - they are easy to put on and take off
    - they are easy to wash and dry
    - they allow the skin to breathe (natural materials are best)
    - there is room to allow for unrestricted movement (to prevent cramping of toes etc.)
    - they are suitable for the time of year
    - for safety reasons, they are free from long ties and ribbons
    - they avoid lacy designs that may catch small fingers
    - they avoid fluffy materials such as mohair, which can get into mouths
    - they are of a suitable length (not too long when crawling etc.).

18. The use of nut oils in baby massage is not recommended, due to links made with the development of nut allergies. Many specialists recommend the use of organic sunflower oil.

19. The use of talcum powder is not recommended for babies as the fine dust can trigger asthma in some infants.

Glossary of terms

active, acquired immunity   immunity acquired through the administration of a live vaccine, e.g. polio.

active, natural immunity   immunity acquired through actually having a condition, e.g. chickenpox.

amnion   the inner layer of the amniotic sac.

amniotic fluid   the fluid in which the developing embryo/foetus floats.

amniotic sac   the muscular bag in which the embryo/foetus develops, made up of two layers: the chorion and the amnion.

anterior fontanelle   a diamond-shaped area of the skull where the bony plates have not yet fused together. It is positioned near to the front of the skull and closes over by 18 months.

antibodies   these protect individuals from infection. Babies receive some antibodies from their mothers (see passive, natural immunity).

attachment   the close relationship between an infant and one or more carers. Also referred to as 'bonding'.

autosomal dominant transference   where a genetically inherited condition has a one in two chance of being passed on to the child.

autosomal recessive transference   where a genetically inherited condition has a one in four chance of being passed on to the child.

bonding   the close relationship between an infant and one or more carers.

caesarian delivery   the delivery of an infant following a surgical incision into the mother's abdominal wall.

caudal   making reference to the lower part of the body.

centile charts   a set of charts recording the growth rate of babies and young children. Also known as 'percentile charts'.

cephalo   referring to the head.

chorion   the outer layer of the **amniotic sac**.

CMN (congenital melanocytic naevus)   a large, often unsightly mole.

colostrum   a yellowish fluid produced from the mother's nipples in the first few days or hours following birth, and preceding the production of milk.

development   the changes that take place as a child grows.

distal   referring to parts of the body at a distance from the central point.

echolalia   where the child focuses on the last word or sound of a word that they have heard spoken.

ectoderm   the outer layer of the neural tube, forming skin, brain and nerves.

embryo   the term used between the third and eighth weeks and of pre-natal development.

endoderm   the most central layer of the neural tube, forming lungs, stomach and intestines.

epidural   a form of pain relief during labour, administered through a catheter into the mother's spinal area.

fine physical skills   hand–eye coordination and manipulative dexterity.
flexed posture   the curled-up position favoured by many babies in the first few days after birth.
flexion   the term used to describe tension in an infant's limbs
foetal position   the curled-up position still favoured by many babies in the first few days after birth.
foetus   the term used from eight weeks' gestation onwards. Everything the infant will have at birth has now been developed and the foetal stage is mostly one of growth.
fontanelles   areas of the skull where bony plates meet. These allow for some movement during the birth process.
forceps   flat tongs used to assist in the delivery of some infants.

genotype   the complete genetic inheritance of an individual.
gestation   the term used to state the length of pregnancy, i.e. 40 weeks' gestation.
gross physical skills   large body movements, including balance and coordination.
Guthrie test   a blood test taken from the infant's heel at around seven or eight days, testing for PKU (phenylketonuria) and hypothyroidism.

herd immunity   vaccination of a sufficiently large proportion of society to drastically reduce the likelihood of being infected by a condition.
hydrocephalus   an unusual amount of cerebrospinal fluid in the brain.

immunisation   a process of vaccination of children to help prevent illness and to eradicate certain conditions from society.
implantation   when the fertilised ovum has implanted itself in the wall of the uterus.
innate   the term used to suggest that something is natural and present at birth.
language acquisition device (LAD   the notion that some knowledge of language is inherent in the brain of a child.
lanugo   a soft, downy hair covering the unborn infant, which follows the whorl patterns of the infant's skin surface.
locomotor skills   large body movements where the individual moves from place to place, e.g. running, hopping, walking.

manipulative skills   fine skills involving dexterity and hand-eye coordination.
meconium   the first stools passed by the infant. Dark greenish black in colour and with a sticky tar-like consistency.
mesoderm   the second layer of the **neural tube**, forming heart, blood, bones, 'sinewy' bits and umbilical cord.
milia   small white spots often seen on newborn babies. Often known as 'milk spots'.
Mongolian blue spot   a dark birthmark mostly found at the base of the spinal area of dark-skinned infants.
Motherese   a higher and slower form of speech often used when communicating with babies.

neonate   the term used to describe an infant during the first month of life.
neural tube   formed from the end of the third week of pregnancy, as the central nervous system of an embryo starts to develop. It is made up of three layers: **ectoderm**, **mesoderm** and **endoderm**.
non-locomotor skills   large body movements made while remaining stationary, e.g. bending.
normative development   the expected rate of development, as an average.

object permanence   an ability to understand that an object exists even though it cannot be seen, and to find objects that have been partially hidden.
observation   the skill of watching in an informed way.
optimum   as good as is possible, e.g. optimum conditions for development.

palmar grasp   the grasping of an object using the whole hand.

parameter   a limit or boundary.

passive, acquired immunity   immunity acquired through an immunisation injection, e.g. Meningitis C.

passive, natural immunity   immunity acquired through antibodies crossing the placenta from mother to infant, or through breast-feeding.

phenotype   the visible arrangement of characteristics inherited by individuals from their parents.

pincer grasp   the grasping of an object between the index finger and the thumb.

PKU (phenylketonuria)   test part of the Guthrie (or heel prick) test, carried out around day seven or eight. Phenylketonuria is a rare blood disorder which can be successfully controlled by a strict diet.

port wine mark   a dark red birthmark, often found on the face or neck of an infant.

possetting   when a baby regurgitates a small amount of milk during or after feeds.

posterior fontanelle   a small triangular-shaped area of the skull where the bony plates have not yet fused together. Found at the back of the skull, it closes over within a few weeks after birth.

primitive reflexes   automatic responses. There are many seen in young babies (e.g. stepping, rooting).

prone   the term used when an infant is laid on his tummy.

pro-social behaviour   an infant's seemingly automatic predisposition to relate to other people.

proximal   being close to the central point of the body.

pyrexia   a raised temperature, i.e. above 37.5 °C (99.5 °F).

rooting   an instinctive searching for the mother's breast by an infant.

SCBU (special care baby unit)   a specialist unit which cares for premature and ill young babies.

separation anxiety   where an infant is distressed at being apart from his main carers.

small for dates   where an infant is below the expected weight for a full-term baby.

stork bites   tiny red birthmarks found on the eyelids, top of the nose and back of the neck.

strawberry naevus (haemangioma)   a raised birthmark, filled with blood vessels.

supine   the term used when an infant is laid on his back.

theory   an idea, a philosophy.

toxocariasis   an infection that can be contracted from handling pets and pet faeces. It is particularly hazardous to pregnant women.

toxoplasmosis   an infection that can be contracted through raw meat, causing serious birth defects.

treasure basket   a small basket of safe and stimulating objects all made from natural materials.

TSH (thyroid stimulating hormone) test   part of the Guthrie (or heel prick) test, carried out at around day seven. It tests for hypothyroidism, an endocrine disorder. It can be successfully controlled if detected at this early stage.

umbilical stump   once the umbilical cord has been clamped and cut the stump left behind dries up and drops off after a few days.

ventouse suction   delivery of an infant with the aid of a disc-shaped cup and a vacuum pump. The cup is attached to the infant's skull.

vernix caseosa   a creamy white substance covering the infant in the womb, offering protection and lubrication for the skin.

weaning   the transition from milk only feeds to mixed feeding.

winding   the method used to help an infant bring up excess air swallowed while feeding.

X-linked transference   where a genetically inherited condition is passed on via the X chromosome.

zygote   the term used for the clump of human 'cells' that develops between conception and implantation.

References and further reading

Cullis, T., Dolan, L. and Groves, D. (1999) *Psychology for You*. Cheltenham: Nelson Thornes.

Dare, A. and O'Donovan, M. (1998) *A Practical Guide to Working With Babies* (2nd edition). Cheltenham: Nelson Thornes.

Fantz, R. L. (1961) 'The origin of form perception', *Scientific American*, 201: 66–72.

Flanagan, C. (1996) *Applying Psychology to Early Child Development*. London: Hodder & Stoughton

Green, S. (2000) *BTEC National Early Years*. Cheltenham: Nelson Thornes.

Green. S. (2002) *BTEC First Early Years*. Cheltenham: Nelson Thornes.

Sheridan, M. (1997) *From Birth to Five Years: Children's Developmental Progress* (7th impression). London: Routledge.

The Learning Centre
S   H TRAFFORD COLLEGE
Manchester Road
West Timperley
Altrincham
Cheshire
WA14 5PQ